Advance Praise for
Kaleidoscope

"A fascinating historical account of a subject that has mostly been treated in biographies. Kato's contextualization of the Uchiyama bookstore offers important insights on Pan-Asian ideas and networks, and reveals the ideological links between groups and events across the span of the Sino-Japanese War (1937-1945) and the years leading up to it. While Sino-Japan relations can be easily haunted by the "history problem," Kato reminds us of another side of the relationship that should be fully acknowledged, one of cooperation and friendship."
— Xia Yun, Professor of History at Shanghai University, College of Liberal Arts

"Dr. Naoko Kato's Kaleidoscope is a positive, human-centered, and beautifully written story of Chinese-Japanese friendship and cultural exchange during an era of intense conflict and war. Fascinating and often inspiring, it reveals up close an unknown part of the history of the Second World War."
— Mark Metzler, Professor of History and International Studies, University of Washington

"Naoko Kato's Kaleidoscope is a fascinating account of the human networks created by Uchiyama Kanzō in Shanghai in the 1920s and 1930s. At a time when Sino-Japanese relations were characterized by growing hostility, Uchiyama's bookstore became a center for intellectual, political, and creative exchange between some of China's leading writers and artists and figures in the Japanese creative and political worlds. Kato's carefully researched and written work provides a window on a long-forgotten world and the role of Uchiyama in promoting Sino-Japanese friendship from the 1920s to the 1950s."

— Linda Grove, Professor Emerita, Sophia University

KALEIDOSCOPE

The Uchiyama Bookstore and its Sino-Japanese Visionaries

Shanghai Uchiyama Bookstore
上海内山書店

Naoko Kato

Kaleidoscope

The Uchiyama Bookstore and its Sino-Japanese Visionaries

By Naoko Kato

ISBN-13: 978-988-8769-64-3

© 2022 Naoko Kato

HISTORY / Asia

EB172

All rights reserved. No part of this book may be reproduced in material form, by any means, whether graphic, electronic, mechanical or other, including photocopying or information storage, in whole or in part. May not be used to prepare other publications without written permission from the publisher except in the case of brief quotations embodied in critical articles or reviews. For information contact info@earnshawbooks.com

Published by Earnshaw Books Ltd. (Hong Kong)

DEDICATION

To my parents, Emiko and Haruichi Kato

Contents

Note on Romanization and Ideograms	1
Why a Kaleidoscope?	2
Introduction	3
1. A Christian Bookstore (1875-1917)	7
2. Pan-Asian Dreams (1878-1913)	17
3. A Sino-Japanese Bookstore (1917-1924)	34
4. A Sino-Japanese Cultural Salon (1926-1930)	52
5. A Haven (1927-1936)	76
6. Searching for Peace Amidst War (1925-1945)	105
7. Japan-China Friendship Association (1945-1959)	125
8. Epilogue	155
Main Characters	160
Timeline	166
Acronyms	176
Map of the Uchiyama Bookstore Neighborhood	177
Author's Note	178
Major Works Cited	179
Photo Credits	183
Acknowledgments	184
About the Author and Editor	185
Index of Names	187

Note on Romanization and Ideograms

CHINESE PERSONAL names, names of publications, places, streets, events, and other nouns are rendered in the pinyin system of romanization without tone marks. Ideograms for personal names before the adoption of simplified Chinese characters in 1949 are rendered in traditional Chinese characters. Personal names are denoted family name first followed by given name.

Post-1949 street names are used throughout the book. For pre-1949 street names and their correlation with post-1949 street names, see Paul French, *The Old Shanghai A-Z* (Hong Kong: Hong Kong University Press, 2010).

Japanese personal names, names of publications, places, streets, events, and other nouns are rendered in the Hepburn system of romanization. Japanese names are denoted family name first followed by given name.

Why a Kaleidoscope?

KALEIDOSCOPE WAS the journal that Uchiyama Bookstore's Sino-Japanese cultural salon produced during the 1920s and 1930s. As the viewer turns a kaleidoscope, the colored pieces within shift relative to each other and create ever-shifting patterns in which shapes and colors vary in dominance. The kaleidoscope metaphor highlights the multi-functionality that characterizes Uchiyama Kanzō and the Uchiyama Bookstore.

In this book, as each chapter turns into the next, the reader sees the Sino-Japanese network around Uchiyama Bookstore during a particular period. While the mix of characters changes from one chapter to the next, each character maintains a unique identity throughout the story. In eight turns, the kaleidoscope presents the changing zones of Sino-Japanese contact within which Uchiyama and Uchiyama Bookstore functioned during the turbulent first half of the 20th century.

INTRODUCTION

UCHIYAMA KANZŌ 内山完造 (1885-1959) was not a stereotypical Japanese conformist. He was a social activist with a robust sense of personal identity. He was a Christian who lived his faith despite constant accusations by fellow Japanese of being unpatriotic and spying for the Chinese. He was not content to exercise his faith by merely attending church services. His mission was to make a visible difference in the world. To this end, under the growing cloud of nationalism, hostility between Chinese and Japanese people, and war between the two nations, Uchiyama devoted his life to facilitating connections between individual Chinese and Japanese people and ultimately to the furtherance of cross-cultural understanding between the peoples of the two nations. Most significantly, Uchiyama Kanzō humanized the enemy—an activity that took exceptional faith and courage.

Previous monographs on Uchiyama Kanzō and Uchiyama Bookstore have relied almost entirely on Uchiyama's autobiography. In addition, these monographs have focused on Uchiyama's relationship with Lu Xun or the bookstore's role as a cultural salon bringing together Japanese and Chinese literati. All these works present a continuous history of the bookstore based on Uchiyama's life and do not significantly differ from one another.

The bookstore remained constant as a place where customers bought books and gathered to chat with like-minded patrons. However, as the historical context changed, so did the needs of the bookstore's Chinese and Japanese patrons. This book focuses on the changing historical context and how the bookstore's principal function shifted in response.

Uchiyama Bookstore was the fulcrum of a Sino-Japanese "contact zone"[1] of cosmopolitan individuals. Even as their respective nation-states were rife with internal challenges, at war, and without official diplomatic relations, these individuals continued to establish and maintain their relationships. Through the activities of Uchiyama Kanzō and other Sino-Japanese visionaries that emerged around him and Uchiyama Bookstore, this story presents a kaleidoscopic perspective of a particular Sino-Japanese contact zone active between 1875 and 1959.

Except for the work of a few specialists, historians have given little attention to interactions between Chinese and Japanese intellectuals during these periods. During the late Qing period, relationships began to form. They continued to emerge and develop during subsequent overlapping historical periods in China and Japan—China's Republican period (1911-1949), Japan's Taishō period (1912-1926), and the first half of the Shōwa period (1926-1989). Pursued against political odds by a few courageous individuals and organizations, interactions between Chinese and Japanese intellectuals continued beyond the founding on October 1, 1949, of the People's Republic of China (PRC) and into the postwar second half of Japan's Shōwa period. Amidst this tumultuous historical period, Uchiyama Kanzō lived out his Christian mission as a Sino-Japanese cultural liaison. Through his bookstore, May Fourth Chinese revolutionaries, many of whom had studied in Japan, Japanese left-wing activists working for the communist cause, and visiting Japanese writers eager to meet their Chinese counterparts met and formed lifelong relationships.

The shift from wartime to postwar Japan is another blind spot in writings on Japanese history. This narrative assumes a discontinuity between an undemocratic prewar Japan and a democratic postwar Japan. According to this narrative, after its surrender to Allied Forces, war-hungry Japan makes a sudden turn toward democracy, and with Article Nine of its 1947 Constitution, disavows "war as a means to settle international disputes involving the state." This story introduces Japan's wartime peace movements, limited as they were. It traces them back to visionaries whose work laid the foundation that became the Sino-Japanese contact zone for which Uchiyama Bookstore served as a fulcrum.

Sino-Japanese tensions surrounding the "history problem" overemphasize the role of right-wing nationalists and the Japanese state while overlooking the crucial historical role of left-wing Japanese groups. Uchiyama is a key to understanding the ideological connection between prewar Pan Asian antiwar activists and postwar peace activists and "China Hand" diplomats and intellectuals accused in Japan of being the "hands of Red China." On his return to Japan after his deportation from China, Uchiyama was known and valued for his prewar connection with Chinese intellectuals. Consequently, he became one of the founding members of several nongovernmental Sino-Japan organizations, including the Japan-China Friendship Association.

During its years of operation in Shanghai, Uchiyama Bookstore and Uchiyama Kanzō attracted a most unusual combination of Chinese and Japanese cosmopolitans. This ability of Uchiyama and his bookstore to transcend divisions and borders makes this story such an interesting case study of an intercultural contact zone.

KALEIDOSCOPE

Endnotes:

1 Mary Louise Pratt has defined intercultural "contact zones" as "the space of colonial encounters, the space in which peoples geographically and historically separated come into contact with each other and establish ongoing relations." Mary Louise Pratt. *Imperial Eyes: Travel Writing and Transculturation* (London; New York: Routledge, 1992), 6.

First Turn of the Kaleidoscope

A Christian Bookstore
(1875-1917)

In September 1917, a Japanese man in Shanghai named Uchiyama Kanzō put up a paper sign on the front of his house[1] announcing the opening of a book shop. Uchiyama started the business with a beer box containing eighty books ordered from Keiseisha Publishing House, a Tokyo publisher of Christian books. The books that made up the bookstore's initial stock were hymnals, faith diaries, and copies of the Bible. "I opened the box and placed the books on a chest of drawers. However, the books did not look like merchandise, so I created two shelves with some wooden boards and placed that on top of an old desk." Thus, from this humble beginning, Shanghai's Uchiyama Bookstore thrived for thirty years, notwithstanding growing nationalism and antagonism between the people and governments of Japan and China.

KALEIDOSCOPE

If Uchiyama and his wife Miki had been seeking a business opportunity to make a living in Shanghai, they would not have opened a Christian bookstore. Uchiyama was already a successful businessman selling Osaka-based pharmaceutical company Taguchi Santendō's University Eyedrops in China. Instead, by operating a bookstore "on the side," Miki had something to do besides housekeeping during Uchiyama's long business trips. The bookstore also gave the Japanese community access to Japanese language Christian materials.

The Uchiyamas opened their bookstore offering Christian materials during an era when Christianity, Pan-Asianism, and pacifism were among the unifying multinational forces bringing the Japanese and Chinese together. It was also a time when the Japanese government considered Japanese Christians unpatriotic. Uchiyamas' Christian identity set him apart from the larger Japanese community. Because he attended church, Uchiyama did not join his Santendō colleagues in their Sunday group outings and activities. Neither did he participate with business associates in drinking and dining together at the end of workdays. Consequently, his Japanese co-workers at Santendō labeled him unpatriotic and shunned him. Later, during the Second Sino-Japanese War, Uchiyama expressed sympathy for Chinese students' anti-Japanese/pro-Allied activities, further distancing himself from Shanghai's Japanese community. Pursuing such a markedly different lifestyle from his compatriots required great courage and determination.

During the last years of the Qing Dynasty, thousands of young Chinese men studied in Japan on Qing government scholarships. They studied Western works in Japanese translation and returned to China fluent in Japanese. Many brought new ideas out of line with those of the Qing state or Republican China that followed. Leftist Chinese were generally comfortable in Shanghai's Little

Japan. They had Japanese friends there and could readily disappear into the community. With the help of Japanese friends and community leaders, they could even hide out in Little Japan in times when authorities set to rounding up, arresting, and even executing leftist activists and writers. These young men, and others like them living in the foreign concessions and other parts of Shanghai, were drawn to a bookstore that carried books in Japanese. Uchiyama was an astute businessman and recognized the opportunity to serve this market. Throughout its history, Uchiyama Bookstore would stock Christian-related titles. But the bookstore soon began to carry, and ultimately specialize in, secular works, especially Japanese translations of Western works — literature, history, philosophy, politics, law, and medicine.

When Uchiyama Bookstore succeeded as a business, Uchiyama left Santendō and joined Miki in running the bookstore. Between World War I and World War II, Uchiyama Bookstore would evolve into one of Shanghai's most famous bookstores and a magnet for Chinese and Japanese cultural literati. Although it continued to carry Christian-related titles, it was not a Christian bookstore during most of its thirty years of operation. With its foundation in Uchiyama Kanzō's and Miki's Christian faith, the spirit of the bookstore was Christian to its core. However, as it became widely known as Shanghai's preeminent Sino-Japanese cultural salon, most people largely forgot its Christian foundation.

The story of Uchiyama Bookstore grew out of Christian-based roots extending back to Niijima Jō, founder in 1875 of Kyoto's Dōshisha University[2] and the Japanese Congregational Church. Thus, based on his Christian principles, Uchiyama Kanzō formulated his approach to the operation of his bookstore. Moreover, Uchiyama's connection with extensive Japanese-Christian networks facilitated his tireless endeavor to foster personal relationships and build cross-cultural understanding between the Chinese and Japanese people.

Besides differing from most Japanese of his time, Uchiyama Kanzō even deviated from well-known Japanese Protestant Christians. With their educational credentials and samurai family backgrounds, these elite Japanese primarily viewed Protestant Christianity as part of Japan's path to modernization and salvation of the country from the fate of other East Asian countries in the face of Western military might. In contrast, Uchiyama was a "born again" Christian. His conversion to Christianity resembled the biblical story of the Prodigal Son, who wasted his life and then returned home and received his father's forgiveness.

Uchiyama Kanzō was born in 1885 in Yoshii, Okayama prefecture, the eldest of four brothers and three sisters. His father was the village headman and a member of the village assembly. Although a bright student, Uchiyama was a rebel — writing graffiti on the blackboard and ganging up with fellow students against the teacher. His behavior was so unruly that he earned the nickname *shiokara* (the most indelicate translation is "salted fish guts"). At age twelve, the family sent Kanzō and his excess energy to apprentice with an Osaka merchant family. He indulged in gourmet foods paid for with money stolen from his employer. At age sixteen, his boss found Uchiyama out and fired him. He soon found work in a factory, but it did not suit him. He quit and returned to Okayama, stayed awhile, stole money from his father, and ran away to Osaka. Uchiyama had severed all ties with his parents and relatives and was on his own. When his money ran out, Uchiyama went to his former factory boss, who introduced him to an employer in Kyoto.

For the next ten years, Uchiyama worked for a Kyoto textile wholesaler. His boss, who loved to gamble, left Uchiyama in charge of business and the care of his employees. Forced for seventy days to look after the shop assistant ill with typhus, Uchiyama resigned. Later writing in his memoirs, he recalled that his only possessions were 50 *sen* and one futon set (a mattress, a comforter, and a pillow).[3] Instead, unlike the biblical prodigal son, Uchiyama did not return home to receive his father's forgiveness. From this low point, he began a series of life changes that led him to Christianity and his life's mission, the active promotion of peace and friendship between Chinese and Japanese people.

Uchiyama's 1912 encounter with Christianity marked the beginning of the revolutionary turn in his life. On January 31, at the suggestion of Kotani Shōzaburō, a shawl manufacturer and business associate with whom he had chatted about Christianity, Uchiyama knocked on the door of Kyoto Church. The church was unusual for a Japanese Protestant church of the time. Parishioners mainly were merchants who operated shops around central Kyoto's Shijō Street. In contrast, most Christian churches of the time catered to elite members of Japanese society.

Symbolically, as Uchiyama left his meeting with assistant Pastor Itō, he threw his exquisite ivory, gold, and precious stone-decorated tobacco case down into the sewer. After this encounter, although he continued to engage in various odd jobs to support himself, Uchiyama's life revolved around the church. At Kyoto Church, with its connections to Dōshisha University and its founder Niijima Jō, Uchiyama Kanzō laid the foundation for his Christian faith and pacifist mission.

With funds from the Japanese Congregational Church (Nihon kumiai kirisuto kyōkai), in 1875, Niijima Jō founded Dōshisha Western School. His mission in establishing Dōshisha was to "convert, cultivate, and educate individuals for a higher moral and national purpose." Kyoto was not a logical first choice as a location for a Christian educational institution. To unify the country under State Shintoism, eight years before the school's founding, the newly established Meiji government had set out to separate Buddhism from Shintoism. Then in 1873, the government officially lifted its 200-year ban on Christianity. With the promulgation of State Shinto under the Meiji government, the large Buddhist community centered around Kyoto's many temples lost much of the power and privilege it had previously enjoyed. When the ban on Christianity was lifted, Kyoto's Buddhist community was even more marginalized. Consequently, the anti-Christian sentiment was a strong force in Kyoto.

Even so, Niijima's networks led him to Kyoto. Niijima and M.L. Gordon met while students at Amherst College in the USA, a non-sectarian institution "for the classical education of indigent young men of piety and talents for the Christian ministry."[4] Through Niijima, his brother-in-law Yamamoto Kakuma, from an elite samurai family background, met M.L. Gordon, now a Congregational missionary to Japan, and converted to Christianity. Niijima built his school on Kyoto property owned by brother-in-law Yamamoto.

The feudal lords of Kumamoto Prefecture on the island of Kyūshū recruited American educational missionary Leroy Lansing Janes to operate a Western Studies School to promote Western studies and morals. Under the influence of Janes, some thirty of his students converted to Christianity. In 1876, opposition from conservative elements forced Janes to close the school. He and his students relocated to Kyoto and were among Dōshisha's inaugural student body. Speaking to the university's first graduating class, Niijima urged the graduates to put their lives on the line to lead and reform Japan. By 1878, Dōshisha graduates had become significant forces of evangelization in

Japan. They were replacing foreign missionaries, a process Niijima saw as necessary to strengthen Japan's independence from the West.

The growth of the community of Dōshisha graduates led to the 1876 founding of Kyoto's first three churches, and in 1883 to the founding of Kyoto Church, where Uchiyama encountered Christianity, all under the auspices of the Tokyo-based Japanese Congregational Church. Although merchants comprised a significant portion of Kyoto Church membership, the church maintained a strong connection with Dōshisha. Church members studied theology there, and many of its pastors, including Makino Toraji, were Dōshisha graduates influenced by Niijima Jō.

Taguchi Kenkichi, a Kyoto Church member, was the founder of Osaka-based pharmaceutical company Taguchi Santendō. He asked Pastor Makino to find a Christian who would be willing to go to Shanghai and sell the company's University Eyedrops in China.[5] One Sunday in 1913, Pastor Makino pulled Uchiyama aside after worship and asked if he would be interested in going to China to sell pharmaceuticals. At the time, Uchiyama had grown uncomfortable with widespread untruthfulness in the Japanese business community and was ready for a change. Makino persuaded Uchiyama to accept Taguchi's invitation to conduct business where he would not have to lie. Within ten days, Uchiyama exchanged his possessions for a Bible, a hymnal, and copies of Uchimura Kanzō's monthly magazine *Biblical Studies* (*Seisho no kenkyū*). Then on March 20, 1913, Pastor Makino saw Uchiyama off for Shanghai.

Three years later, Taguchi Kenkichi approached Pastor Makino Toraji again and asked him to find a Christian woman willing to marry Uchiyama and go to China. Makino thought of Inoue Mikiko, aka Miki (1893-1945), a member of his Kyoto

Church congregation. Miki's father had put her to work as an entertainer in Kyoto's infamous *Gion* entertainment district. He was a gambler and had gone further and further into debt. He had sacrificed his two daughters to the entertainment trade to raise money. After Miki's sister passed away, the burden of her father's debts rested solely on her shoulders. She began attending Kyoto Church, reading the Bible, and converted to Christianity. When Makino introduced Miki and asked Uchiyama to marry her, Uchiyama did not hesitate, and in 1916, the couple married. It was also Makino who introduced Uchiyama to Keiseisha Publishing House. Tokyo-based, Keiseisha was one of Japan's earliest publishers of Christian materials and supplied all the titles for Uchiyama's new Christian bookstore. Throughout the remainder of Uchiyama's life, Makino Toraji remained his mentor.

Besides Niijima Jō and Makino Toraji, Uchiyama looked to another Christian, Uchimura Kanzō, as his role model. In 1903, just as the Empire of Japan prepared to wage war against the Russian Empire, Uchimura declared his conversion to pacifism and was among Japan's preeminent pre-WWII pacifists. Uchiyama admired Uchimura, who was labeled 'unpatriotic' by his fellow Japanese after his conversion to pacifism. However, despite the stones continually thrown into his house, he bravely held to his belief in the evils of war.

In 1908 Uchimura wrote, "I love two Js—one is Jesus Christ, and the other is Japan; the two Js—Jesus and Japan, which I love more, I do not know. Japanese hate me because I believe in Jesus, and Western missionaries dislike me because I am too Japanese. However, I cannot lose my two Js—Jesus and Japan."[6] On his tomb, he expressed his wish to have these words inscribed:

NAOKO KATO

I for Japan;
Japan for the world;
The world for Christ;
And all for God.

As he set off for Shanghai, Uchiyama carried a Bible, a hymnal, and forty-some back issues of Uchimura Kanzō's monthly magazine. In his memoirs, Uchiyama recalls during his first two years in Shanghai, the Bible, the Psalms, and Uchimura's magazines were his only reading materials.

Like Uchimura, Uchiyama struggled with the ideas expressed in Uchimura's epitaph — how best could a Japanese serve God in China when Japan and China were at war? Through their tireless promotion of Sino-Japanese cultural exchanges, Uchiyama Kanzō and Miki sought to reconcile this contradiction. In Uchiyama's own words, ridding the difference between Japanese and Chinese through the management of my bookstore — this was my belief in God. It is not true faith if we cannot believe in our brothers or sisters. The starting point of faith comes from believing in people; hence I believed in my customers and let them take care of the rest. If I were to add another thing, it is that success or no success is in the hands of God. Behind this is the simple belief in working faithfully. When we realized these things, the Sino-Japanese cultural exchange came into being.[7]

Influenced by his Christian mentors and in the context of practicing his Christian faith, Uchiyama Kanzō moved to Shanghai in 1913, married Miki in 1916, and in 1917, supported her in opening a makeshift Christian bookstore in their Shanghai home in Weishengli, Lane 1881, North Sichuan Road. The rudimentary bookstore would become Uchiyama Bookstore and salon at 2048 North Sichuan Road, for which Uchiyama Kanzō and Uchiyama Bookstore are known to this day

KALEIDOSCOPE

Endnotes:
1 Weishengli 魏盛里 was located off Lane 1881, North Sichuan Road. Weishengli has been demolished and replaced with modern buildings and Lane 1881 no longer exists.
2 Dōshisha University is a private university in Kyoto City. It was established as Dōshisha English School with the mission of advancing Christian education in Japan. It was granted university status in 1925. Dōshisha is one of Japan's oldest private institutions of higher learning, offering education based on Christian principles.
3 Yoshida Hiroji, *Rojin no tomo Uchiyama Kanzō no shōzō* (Tokyo: Shinkyō Shuppansha, 1994), 64.
4 Amherst College, Amherst, Massachusetts, is the third oldest college in the state. It is one of the premier undergraduate liberal arts colleges in the USA. Based on its historical link, the college maintains a close relationship with Dōshisha University.
5 Santendō Pharmaceutical Company 参天製薬株式会社, Santen seiyaku kabushiki-gaisha was founded 1890 in Osaka by Taguchi Kenkichi. In 1899 the company launched University Eyedrops. Santendō eyedrops were produced from a formulation developed by the Department of Opthalmology at Tokyo Imperial University's affiliated hospital to treat common eye ailments such as pink eye and blurred vision. The privately held Osaka-based company, now known as Santen, has the largest share within the Japanese ophthalmic market and is one of the world's leading suppliers of ophthalmic pharmaceuticals.
6 Uchimura Kanzō, *Representative Men of Japan: Essays* (Tokyo: Keiseisha, 1921).
7 Uchiyama Kanzō, *Sonhē ōhe: Shanhai seikatsu sanjūgonen* (Tokyo: Iwanami Shinsho, 1949), 13.

Second Turn of the Kaleidoscope

Pan-Asian Dreams
(1878-1913)

ALONG WITH CHRISTIANITY, Pan-Asianism was a unifying force that brought Chinese and Japanese together at Uchiyama Bookstore. Pan-Asianism was primarily an anti-Western movement that emphasized Asian solidarity. Leaders of non-Western countries began to explore alternative visions of a new world order based on Pan-Asian internationalism. The 1905 victory of Japan over Russia in the Russo-Japanese War demonstrated that the West was no longer invincible. With Japan's rapid modernization and triumph over a Western nation in war, its confidence grew relative to other Asian countries. The Asian Monroe Doctrine, which claimed Japan's leadership role in Asia, began to incorporate Pan-Asianism.

As Japan increasingly turned toward nationalism and imperialism, shared visions of Pan-Asianism became challenging to sustain with its Asian neighbours. Nevertheless, Uchiyama held to the Pan-Asian dream of Japanese solidarity with the Chinese, sharing a common civilization, and felt betrayed by Japan's aggressive shift.

During its 220-year policy of *sakoku* (locked country), the Tokugawa shogunate continued relations with Northeast Asian countries—Korea, China, and the Ryūkyū Kingdom. As a result, scholars of Chinese Studies who were well versed in Confucian studies and classical Chinese imported Western knowledge through publications in China. Tokugawa-era Japanese castaways such as John Manjirō (Nakahama Manjirō 1827-1898) were also important sources of knowledge from the outside world. John Manjirō, for instance, spent a decade in the United States, and spread his knowledge about the West to leading figures such as Sakamoto Ryōma (1836-1867) who would come to overthrow the Tokugawa shogunate through the Meiji Restoration.

At the same time, the shogunate imposed strict regulations on commerce, allowing only Chinese and Dutch merchants to trade in Nagasaki through the island of Dejima. Part of the purpose was to sever ties with European countries that had become active in China and posed a potential military threat. The resumption of Christian proselytizing was also a threat to shogunate authority. Through the Dutch enclave in Dejima, a small number of Japanese scholars developed "Dutch Learning," focused mainly on natural sciences such as medicine, but also including map-making and military science. Consequently, substantial knowledge of the West deepened over time. The Dutch in Dejima, a foreign trading post on a small manmade island Nagasaki harbor, had even informed the Japanese that Commodore Matthew C. Perry's (1794-1858) expedition was on its way.[1] As a result, leaders were well aware of the political, scientific, and industrial revolutions that had changed the Western world even during the country's two centuries of so-called seclusion.

In 1854, under coercion by Commodore Perry and his heavily armed fleet, the Tokugawa shogunate ratified the Peace and Amity Treaty with the U.S. and the Anglo-Japanese Friendship Treaty with the United Kingdom. The treaties established formal diplomatic relations with the two countries and opened the ports of Shimoda and Hakodate to American and British vessels. The treaties also ended measures that had barred nearly all foreign nationals from entering Japan and prevented ordinary Japanese from leaving the country. As a result, Japanese began traveling to the United States, the United Kingdom, and Europe to pursue Western-style education. In addition, western-educated Japanese began translating modern Western titles into Japanese. Translations into both English and Japanese by China-based Protestant missionaries also began arriving in Japan. Thus, Western titles in translation, especially in the fields of law, the sciences, and medicine, became highly sought after in both China and Japan.

Rather than proselytizing directly in China, many Protestant missionaries provided Western education, state-of-the-art medical care, and Chinese translations of Western works. Moreover, while China's dominant Protestant sponsored publishing house, Shanghai-based American Presbyterian Mission Press,[2] published religious titles, non-religious titles dominated its output. For example, in 1866, American medical missionary Dr. James Curtis Hepburn (1815-1911) and Japanese scholar of classical Chinese, Kishida Ginkō 岸田吟香 (1833-1905), joined forces to compile and published the first Japanese-English dictionary at American Presbyterian Mission Press. The dictionary rapidly became the standard reference for Chinese students studying Japanese.

In 1863 Kishida, suffering from a severe eye ailment, traveled from Tokyo to Yokohama to see Dr. Hepburn, who operated a medical clinic there. Hepburn's Western eyedrops formulation rapidly cleared the infection. The patient-doctor relationship evolved into Kishida and Hepburn's collaboration on the dictionary. Furthermore, through Hepburn, Kishida met and became a close friend of Joseph Heco (1837-1897), who was a castaway; met Heco's friend Eugene Miller Van Reed (1835-1873), and Hepburn's English language student Honma Senzō 本間潜蔵 (1843-1923).[3] Kishida began his involvement in Japan's earliest Western-style journalism with these men.

In 1865, Kishida assisted Heco and Honma in launching *Kaigai Shinbun* (*Overseas News*). The newspaper, written in everyday Japanese, was the first non-government-controlled newspaper produced in Japan. Printed in large quantities under Yokohama's extraterritoriality status, the newspaper specialized in news from the West gleaned from the crew and passengers of ships arriving at the Port of Yokohama. Simultaneously, Kishida and Hepburn began their three-year collaboration on the Japanese-English dictionary.

In 1868, Kishida and Van Reed launched one of Japan's earliest Western-style Japanese language newspapers, *Yokohama shinpō moshihogusa* (*Yokohama News Anthology*). Then, in 1873, *Tōkyō nichinichi shinbun* (*Tokyo Daily News*), established the previous year, hired Kishida as its "principal writer." He went with Imperial forces to report on Japan's Taiwan Expedition of 1875. The newspaper published twenty-eight installments of Kishida's "News from Taiwan" column. Thus, he became Japan's first foreign war correspondent and sparked an interest in the Japan-China relationship that drew him to do business in China.[4]

The Japanese-English dictionary was a commercial success. However, instead of monetary compensation, Dr. Hepburn taught Kishida to make the formulation for treating common eye ailments and granted him manufacturing and commercialization rights. With personal experience of the efficacy of the solution, together with his ability as a journalist to shape public opinion, in 1875, Kishida opened Rakuzendō 楽善堂 (Hall of Virtuous Delights), a pharmacy in the Ginza district of Tokyo that sold Japan's first Western formulation for treating common eye ailments.[5] Rakuzendō was famous for its effective use of newspaper advertisements. In 1880, Kishida opened Rakuzendō on Henan Middle Road in Shanghai's International Settlement[6] and, in the 1880s, opened branches in the cities of Fuzhou and Hankou—now part of the city of Wuhan.

Besides eyedrops, Rakuzendō stocked books imported from Japan, including English and Japanese language translations of Western medical titles. In addition, Kishida self-published and carried a series of pocket-size editions of Chinese classics popular with candidates for the Chinese civil service examination. These sold more than 150,000 copies per year and launched Kishida in the publishing business. Kishida also published maps and topographies of China and a magazine dedicated to spreading health and Western medical knowledge.

Shenbao (*Shanghai News*) established a column called Gindan (Kishida's literary circle) featuring works of contemporary Chinese poets. Then, in 1888, Kishida turned his second-floor office at the Shanghai Rakuzendō into a venue for regular gatherings of cultural literati over cups of *sake*. Wang Tao, the editor of *Shenbao*, named the 100-member group the Magnolia Poetry-Making Company (Gyokuran-ginsha). Rakuzendō was a huge success. But rather than spending on a lavish lifestyle or sending money back to Japan, Kishida plowed his profits back into Chinese society and earned his business the nickname "Kishida's One-Way Trade."

Kishida Ginkō blazed the trail which Uchiyama Kanzō and

future generations of Japanese would follow to China. Although Kishida got to Shanghai three decades before Uchiyama Kanzō and died years before Uchiyama's arrival, the two shared much in common: both were from Okayama prefecture and lived in Shanghai; both were skilled marketers who sold books and eyedrops; and both hosted cultural salons in their places of business. If Uchiyama had not heard of Kishida before coming to Shanghai, once in Shanghai, he would have learned of Kishida, Rakuzendō, and Kishida's chief disciple Arao Sei.[7]

Though many Japanese were going to the West to study, Arao chose to go to China. When asked why China, he replied, "everyone's hearts seem to be consumed by the West, and nobody reconsiders the importance of our neighbor China. That is why I choose to go to China."[8] In 1886, the Japanese Imperial Army General Staff Headquarters sent First Lieutenant Arao Sei on a spy mission to China. He arranged with Kishida to use the Rakuzendō branch in the city of Hankou[9] as a cover for his work toward his primary goal—reform of China. Between 1886 and 1889, with cover as a Rakuzendō employee, he gathered information on Chinese geography, transportation, industries, trade habits, and commercial goods.

Arao believed that China was of primary importance to Japan. If the West were to gain control of China, Japan would be in grave danger. Through trade, he thought Japan could strengthen its economic position. Both nations would then be better able to contend with the West. In 1890, he retired from the army. With Nezu Hajime, a fellow retired army officer, and the financial backing and support of the Japanese Army General Staff Headquarters, he established the Shanghai-based Research Institute for Sino-Japanese Trade (RISJT). The goal of RISJT was to teach the Chinese language and relevant Chinese commerce courses to Japanese students.[10] RISJT was nominally a market-oriented information gathering and economic analysis unit that became the base of Japanese intelligence activities in China. However, with the 1894 onset of the First Sino-Japanese War, the General Staff ended financial support, and RISJT closed.

Japan had been one of dynastic China's many tributary states, shared a common written language, and was viewed by both Japanese and Chinese as within the sphere of Chinese civilization. However, the Tokugawa shogunate did not participate in the Chinese tributary system, and refused to recognize China's superiority. In the late Tokugawa period, China's status declined relative to the Western powers, and Japanese nativist scholars were eager to distinguish Japan from China. Accordingly, these scholars began replacing China with Japan as the symbolic 'central flower.'

Following the precedent set by Western nations, early in the Meiji period, the government requested a diplomatic treaty. In 1873, Japan and China signed the first treaty between the two countries, Sino-Japanese Friendship and Trade Treaty. Consequently, China began to see Japan as a treacherous barbarian in violation of its tributary state obligations.[11] It was becoming clear that Japan was no longer an extension of Chinese culture, and that Japan was abandoning (Chinese) civilization for Western universalism. At the same time, Western powers rejected Meiji leaders' repeated efforts to be integrated into the global community. Consequently, Meiji leaders became increasingly aware of their cultural and racial identity as Asians. Moreover, although many intellectuals had studied in the West and become specialists in many fields of Western knowledge, they began to sense the limits of Japanese Westernization.

By the mid-1890s, with the spread of Pan-Asian thought, Chinese intellectuals began to acknowledge that Japan and China shared a civilization—they were *tongwen* (same culture/

civilization).¹² Huang Zunxian 黃遵憲 (1848-1905), a Chinese diplomat, scholar, and poet, exemplified the *tongwen* spirit. Early in his career, he served as secretary to the Chinese embassy in Tokyo, where he came to view Japan's simplicity and natural beauty as an idealized ancient China. The concept of cultural affinity was a powerful argument supporting Qing reformers and their ideas. Meiji era *shishi* (men of high purpose) such as ultranationalist Tōyama Mitsuru 頭山満 (1855-1944), politician Inukai Tsuyoshi 犬養毅 (1855-1932), and revolutionary activist Miyazaki Tōten 宮崎滔天 (1871-1922), shared Sun Yat-sen's resentment of Western imperialism. The leaders of the Qing-era Hundred Days of Reform movement, Kang Youwei 康有為 (1958-1927), Liang Qichao 梁啟超 (1873-1929), and Huang Zunxian exalted their Japanese *shishi* counterparts for their part in the success of the Meiji Restoration.¹³ While viewing China as the only civilization and the source from which modern Japan emerged, some Chinese intellectuals began to project Japan as the new leader of Asia.

In 1898, to encourage Chinese students to study in Japan, Qing officials promoted the concept of *tongzhong*. The concept evolved from *tongwen* to include a shared sense of oppression by Western powers. As a result, Chinese students began going to Japan in ever-increasing numbers to learn from the Japanese—commencing in 1896 with thirteen students and by 1906 growing to a peak of 8,000 students. Mutual interest was also a factor. China's Qing government lacked financial resources and human capital to actualize its 1901 educational edict and approached the Meiji government to provide China with teachers and textbooks. Consequently, Japan sent teachers and academic advisors to China, ranging from 148 to 549 per year. These trends grew out of steady, though moderate, late Qing reforms that initiated extensive educational, military, and legal system changes.

Japan provided China with quick access to Western technology. Still, more significantly, it served as a model for the cultural and organizational change that China might emulate. For Japan, with its pride as the first Asian nation to join the ranks of Western powers, strengthening national security reinforced its confidence and hinged, at least in part, on improving relations with China and gaining concession rights alongside Western nations.

After RISJT closed in 1894, Arao Sei and Nezu Hajime joined forces with Konoe Atsumaro (1863-1904), a Pan-Asianist heir to the high-ranking Konoe family of pre-Meiji court nobility. They were determined to create an institution that united China and Japan to promote Sino-Japanese understanding and trade in the *tongwen* spirit. To this end, Konoe, then president of the House of Peers, initiated the founding of the East Asia Common Culture Association, with Nezu Hajime as Secretary-General. In 1900, the Association launched its educational arm, the East Asia Common Culture Academy (EACCA), with Nezu as Headmaster.

Arao's RISJT and its successors, the East Asia Common Culture Association, and the Association's educational arm EACCA, as their names imply, each embodied the *tongwen* spirit. EACCA received funding from the Japanese Ministry of Foreign Affairs as part of the ministry's support of nongovernmental initiatives. The goal of EACCA was to strengthen China and establish Sino-Japanese cooperation in business and trade. It recruited students from prefectures around Japan and became Japan's largest higher education institution outside the country.

Focusing first on language learning, EACCA trained students to be competent in the modern Chinese economy, education, geography, society, politics, and language. In addition, EACCA was known for its annual two-to six-month student research trips throughout China funded by the Japanese Ministry of Foreign Affairs. The East Asia Common Cultural Association published the data from the research trips, including an 11,000-page report titled, *A Comprehensive Book on the Economics Conditions in China*, and submitted it to the General Staff of the Imperial Army, the Ministry of Foreign Affairs, and the Ministry of Agriculture and Commerce.

Graduates were highly sought-after by the Japanese military and Japanese intelligence services for their language skills and in-depth knowledge of China. Furthermore, because of Nezu's connections with Chinese provincial governors gained through the field trip program, many EACCA graduates became teachers and educational advisors for China's modern schools. In later chapters, EACCA students will be among customers of Uchiyama Bookstore.

Like many Pan-Asianists, Arao believed that the First Sino-Japanese War against the corrupt Manchu-dominated Qing was a just war. But, unfortunately, many Japanese graduates he had nurtured at EACCA and who joined the war effort as interpreters lost their lives. At the end of the war, Arao retreated to Nyakuōji Shrine, a Shintō shrine in Kyoto, to mourn the loss of many EACCA graduates and contemplate his next step. He realized if Japan retained control of the Chinese port city of Weihaiwei, captured during the war, and demanded reparations, it would fuel hostility of the Chinese people toward Japan and make achieving economic cooperation more difficult. This view, which he published, marked a shift in his thinking toward an ideology that viewed Japan as the natural leader of the Pan-Asian movement:

> Western and Eastern cultures distinguish the two continents of Europe and Asia: White and yellow constitute two fundamentally different races. The so-called "Eastern advance of Western power" must

surely mean a clash between the two. Therefore, the frailty of Korea should be deeply lamented, not for what it means for Korea, but for what it means for our country. The senility of the Qing Dynasty, no matter what it means for (the Chinese), should be sharply deplored for what it means to (Japan). We must stand together as three countries and rely on each other, staking our domestic order and national prestige before the whole world, to show reverence to the supreme morality of our Imperial Ancestors. We must aid those who are weak, assist those who have become relics, and thus reverse the decline of East Asia.[14]

While a fifteen or sixteen-year-old student at Dōshisha University, Makino was responsible for organizing lectures and hosting visitors. Acting in this capacity, Makino traveled from Kyoto to Osaka to visit Arao at an inn where he was staying and delivered an invitation for Arao to lecture at Dōshisha. Arao agreed on the spot to give three lectures at the university.

Shortly after the First Sino-Japanese War, Makino traveled to Kyoto to visit the grave of his former teacher Niijima Jō, on Mount Nyakuōji.[15] Makino had learned that Arao was staying at Nyakuōji shrine. Since the shrine was a short walk down the mountain from the cemetery, Makino stopped to pay his respects and engaged in a conversation that would shape his subsequent life path. During the visit, Makino told Arao of his wish to go to China. Arao's initial response was negative. Makino then asked Arao if he had studied Christianity. Arao replied that he had not. However, recalling Niijima's lectures at Dōshisha had inspired him to come to Nyakuōji shrine.

For two hours, Makino talked to Arao about Christianity. After patiently listening, Arao replied, "everyone has his mission in life—mine is the China problem, and yours is Christian evangelism. Because you expressed interest in the China problem, I assumed that you would be working with us toward that end. My assumption was wrong. I would happily send you off to China (to evangelize)."[16] Makino did not go to China, but he did become a Congregational Church pastor. As Pastor of Kyoto Church, Makino inspired Uchiyama Kanzō to accept Taguchi Kenkichi's invitation to represent Santendō in China, introduced Uchiyama to his future wife Miki, and served as Uchiyama's lifelong mentor.

Uchiyama Bookstore grew from a sideline into Uchiyama's full-time work, serving Japanese and Chinese customers. He viewed his role as twofold: to show China Japan's strength achieved under the Meiji Restoration and assist China in creating its own new culture. In his memoir *Kakōroku*, Uchiyama expresses his dream for the bookstore:

Our dream was to become the best bookstore in China. As the number of shop assistants increased, we also needed to increase the number of branches. Our dream was to have Uchiyama Bookstores in Guangdong, Beiping (Beijing), and Hankou (Wuhan). Our dream expanded, and we wanted to have our bookstore in each province. We aimed to show China the strength of Japanese culture and help China create its new culture. Unfortunately, when my bookstore was requisitioned, my thirty-year dream became the victim of Japanese militarism and invasion and was shattered.[17]

Uchiyama's "thirty-year dream" was a reference to the 1903 autobiography of Miyazaki Tōten, titled, *My Thirty-three Years' Dream*.[18] Tōten, a revolutionary, had met Sun Yat-sen in 1897 while Sun was in exile in Japan following his failed 1895 revolt. Sun and Miyazaki planned and procured arms from Japan for the 1900 Huizhou Uprising, which also failed. Thus, the Chinese revolution he had worked for thirty-three years to achieve failed, shattering his long-held dream.[19]

Uchiyama penned his "thirty years" piece in April 1947, eight months before his deportation from China. Most striking is his sense of victimization—that Japan's militarism had shattered his dreams. Despite acknowledging his role in "showing China the strength of Japanese culture," Uchiyama did not identify with Japanese militarism. Instead, he identified with the Japanese, who held to the Pan-Asian dream of regional identity as Asians. A sense of being a victim of Japan's militarism while at the same time advocating for Pan-Asianism may appear contradictory to those who equate Pan-Asianism with Japanese expansion and imperialism. However, Uchiyama based his Pan-Asianism on a sense he shared with the Chinese as a victim of Japan's official imperialism.

From the beginning of his life and work in Shanghai, Uchiyama Kanzō considered Chinese people to be his compatriots. As early as 1900, years before his conversion to Christianity and his move to China, Uchiyama dreamed of throwing himself into the Chinese revolution.[20] In China, Uchiyama devoted himself to work on behalf of Santendō and traveled throughout China, promoting the company's University Eyedrops. His autobiography described how he lived like a "Japanese coolie" alongside the Chinese as he traveled China promoting Santendō's product. As he traveled, he often sang his version of a famous military song titled "Senyū" ("Compatriot"). The piece, composed during the Russo-Japanese War in Manchuria, was a requiem to a fallen soldier. Uchiyama's version replaced the word "Manchuria" with "Shanghai" and retained its theme, a powerful sense of solidarity among compatriots.

In May 1915, the Republic of China under Beijing warlord Yuan Shikai accepted most of the Empire of Japan's Twenty-One

Demands.[21] The Twenty-One Demands extended Japan's control over Shandong Province and Manchuria, among other equally harsh terms. As a result, a spontaneous nationwide boycott of Japanese-operated businesses and Japanese-made goods broke out.

At the time, Uchiyama was in Hunan Province carrying a banner advertising University Eyedrops. He was swept up in a crowd of parading coolies. A mob of students joined the parade carrying banners and shouting slogans: "Down with Japanese Imperialism!" "Reject the Twenty-One Demands!" "Commemoration of National Humiliation!" In his autobiography, Uchiyama wrote that he still did not know how he managed to pass through the crowd uneventfully. The uneasy coexistence of the University Eyedrops banner promoting a Japanese product that was an effective cure for a widespread eye ailment, and the anti-Japanese protests, are symbolic of the complex nature of Sino-Japanese relations within which Uchiyama operated in China.

NAOKO KATO

Endnotes:

1 John W. Dower, "Black Ships & Samurai: Commodore Perry and the Opening of Japan (1853-1854)," (Massachusetts Institute of Technology Visualizing Cultures, 2010), https://visualizingcultures.mit.edu/black_ships_and_samurai/pdf/bss_essay.pdf.

2 American Presbyterian Mission Press (China) was established in Macao in 1844, moved to Ningbo in 1845 and Shanghai in 1860. Its operations included printing and publishing, a foundry, and trade in stationery supplies. It grew into the largest and most sophisticated Protestant missionary-operated press in China.

3 Todd S. Munson, *The Periodical Press in Treaty-Port Japan: Conflicting Reports from Yokohama, 1861-1870.* Leiden: Brill, 2013, Introduction and Chapters 1 and 2. Hamada Hikozō 浜田彦蔵(Joseph Heco, 1837-1897) was cast adrift, rescued by an American ship, and put ashore in San Francisco. Hamada learned English, converted to Catholicism, changed his name to Joseph Heco, and was the first Japanese naturalized as a citizen of the USA. Heco met Eugene Miller Van Reed (1835-1873) in San Francisco in 1853, and inspired Van Reed to learn Japanese and "consider commercial possibilities in the orient." In the 1860s, Van Reed becomes known for his recruitment efforts of Japanese immigrants to Hawaii.

4 Matthew Fraleigh, "Japan's First War Reporter: Kishida Ginkō and the Taiwan Expedition," *Japanese Studies*, 30, no.1, (2010), 1.

5 Zinc sulfate was the active ingredient. The website of Eisai Pharmaceutical Company Museum http://www.eisai.co.jp/museum/information/topics/topics14_07.html According to instructions included with the eyedrops called Seikisui (Pure Water), they were for treatment of various eye ailments including pink eye and blurred vision. Webpage. http://jmapps.ne.jp/newspark/det.html?data_id=18834

6 Rakuzendō 楽善堂 Shanghai branch was located at the southeast corner of Henan Middle Road and Jiujiang Road near Nanjing East Road. Kinouchi Makoto ed., *Shanhai rekishi gaido mappu* [Shanghai History Guide Map], (Tokyo: Taishūkan Shoten, 2011), 4.

7 Douglas R. Reynolds, "Training Young China Hands: Tōa Dōbun Shoin and Its Precursors, 1886-1945" in *The Japanese Informal Empire in China, 1895-1937*, ed. Ramon H. Meyers Peter Duus, and Mark R. Peattie (Princeton, New Jersey: Princeton University Press, 1989), 213.

8 Chen Zu En, *Shanhai ni ikita nihonjin: Bakumatsu kara haisen made*, (Tokyo: Taishūkan Shoten, 2010), 85.

9 In 1949 the cities of Wuchang, Hankou (Hankew), and Hanyang, at the confluence of Yangtze River and its largest tributary, the Han River merged to become the city of Wuhan.

10 Fogel, *Articulating the Sinophere: Sino-Japanese Relations in Space and Time*, (Cambridge, Mass.: Harvard University Press, 2009), 95.

11 Douglas Howland. *Borders of Chinese Civilization: Geography and History at Empire's End*. (Durham: Duke University Press, 1996), 43.

12 Rebecca Karl, "Creating Asia: China in the World at the Beginning of the Twentieth Century," *The American Historical Review* 103, no. 4 (1998): 1102.

13 Marius Jansen, *The Japanese and Sun Yat-Sen*, (Cambridge: Harvard University Press, 1954), 66.

14 Michael Schneider, "Kōa-Raising Asia: Arao Sei and Inoue Masaji," in *Pan-Asianism: A Documentary History*, ed. Sven Saaler and Christopher Szpilman (Plymouth: Rowman & Littlefield, 2011), 71.

15 Now known as Dōshisha Cemetery, it contains more than 30 people with connections to Dōshisha University.

16 Makino Toraji, *Hara no ari kara*, (Tokyo: Makino Toraji Sensei Beiju Kinenkai, 1958), 46.
17 Uchiyama Kanzō, *Kakōroku*, (Tokyo: Iwanami Shoten, 1960), 325.
18 Miyazaki Tōten, *My Thirty-Three Years' Dream: The Autobiography of Miyazaki Tōten* (Princeton: Princeton University Press, 1982).
19 Marius Jansen, *The Japanese and Sun Yat-Sen* (Cambridge: Harvard University Press, 1954).
20 Uchiyama Kanzō, *Kakōroku*, 25.
21 Twenty-One Demands of January 18, 1915 was made during WWI by the Empire of Japan on the Republic of China represented at the time by Beijing warlord Yuan Shikai. The demands included provisions that greatly expanded Japanese control of Manchuria and the Chinese economy.

THIRD TURN OF THE KALEIDOSCOPE

A SINO-JAPANESE BOOKSTORE (1917-1924)

IN THE UCHIYAMAS' small living room, the Christian bookstore soon transitioned into a Sino-Japanese bookstore. Despite Shanghai's anti-Japanese rallies and boycotts, both Japanese — socialists and Christians — and Chinese who had studied in Japan — patronized the bookstore and began to form ties. Moreover, the transition took place within the context of international events and social movements that emerged in the late 1910s and flourished into the early 1920s, including internationalism, nationalism, and China's New Culture Movement. Historian Akira Iriye in his 1997 book *Cultural Internationalism and World Order*, summarizes the history of cultural internationalism: the attempt by liberal political and economic institutions and their philosophers, artists, and scientists to build cultural understanding, cooperation, and a sense of shared values across national borders and nationalities through student exchanges, lectures, and the like.¹

In the mid-1910s, students at Beijing University, many of whom had studied in Japan, began to call for creating a new, more global Chinese culture. On September 15, 1915, Chen Duxiu 陳獨秀 (1879-1942), who would in 1921, with Li Dazhao 李大釗 (1889-1927), cofound the Communist Party of China (CPC), launched the *New Youth* 新青年 magazine. The magazine launched China's New Culture Movement 新文化運動 and quickly became the country's most popular and widely distributed journal. The magazine promoted science, democracy, and vernacular Chinese literature and marked the emergence of nationalism in China. Writers were at the forefront of both the New Culture Movement and Chinese nationalism that grew along with encroachment upon the Chinese Motherland by colonial powers, especially Japan. Professor of humanities Leo Ou-fan Lee in his book *Lu Xun and His Legacy*, contends that modern Chinese writers were the cultural literati of the day. Lee argues that they served as the critical conscience of society and carried the moral burden of uplifting ethical standards and improving their nation.² They wrote in vernacular rather than in classical Chinese and used literary works as weapons to attack traditional Confucian culture, promote New Culture ideas, and create "new" literature to "save" China.³

Pan-Asianism in Japan emerged from internationalism and initially manifested as an Asian regional identity premised on the distinction between Asia and the West. It then evolved into an ideology that extended Japanese nationalism overseas to the West and East Asia.⁴ During private conversations in 1905, U.S. President Theodore Roosevelt suggested to Japanese politician Kaneko Kentarō 金子堅太郎 (1853-1942) that "the future policy of Japan towards Asiatic countries should be like that of the United States toward its neighbors on the American continent as expressed in the Monroe Doctrine of 1823." Roosevelt contended that a Japanese Monroe Doctrine in Asia "would remove the temptation of European encroachment. Japan would be the recognized leader of the Asiatic nations, and her power would form the shield behind which she could reorganize her national system."[5]

In 1921, the Empire of Japan officially claimed special rights in East Asia. On January 21, Minister of Foreign Affairs Uchida Kōsai 内田康哉 (1865-1936) delivered a report to the General Assembly of the League of Nations. The report stated that Japan was entitled to special rights in East Asia, comparable to those the U.S claimed in the Western Hemisphere under the Monroe Doctrine.[6] In fact, under its Twenty-One Demands of 1915, Japan had already greatly extended its control over Manchuria and the Chinese economy.

During a January 1918 address to U. S. Congress on war aims and peace terms, president Woodrow Wilson laid out his Fourteen Points—principles for peace which he proposed to bring to peace negotiations at the end of WWI. Promulgating internationalism, Wilson's Fourteen Points included creating the League of Nations and establishing the right to self-determination and self-government for nations large and small. This idea gained momentum among anti-colonial nationalists in colonized countries who claimed that non-White peoples also had the right to self-determination.[7]

At the end of WWI, delegates from around the world assembled at the Paris Peace Conference of 1919-1920 to set peace terms for the defeated central powers and establish norms for ensuring peace in the post-war period. On behalf of the Japanese government, diplomat Makino Nobuaki 牧野伸顕 (1861-1949) proposed adding a racial equality clause to the covenant establishing the League of Nations. He asserted that "men of different races had fought together on the Allied side during the war, leading to a common bond of sympathy and gratitude never before experienced."[8] The Japanese intended to secure equality for their nationals and equality for the League of Nations members.[9] But the proposed clause challenged the established norms of the Western-dominated international system with its colonial rule over non-white people and was ultimately rejected.[10]

The Paris Peace Conference revoked most of Japan's Twenty-One Demands on China. Still, it upheld the transfer of Germany's former concessions in Shandong Province to Japan. Then, on May 4, 1919, patriotic feelings and the zeal for reform erupted in China in what would become known as the May Fourth Movement. A mass demonstration by 3,000 students broke out in Beijing. It rapidly spread to other cities nationwide, where industrialists, merchants, and workers joined forces with students. The demonstrators protested Japanese imperialism, unequal treatment of China by the Western powers at the Peace Conference, and the representatives of the Beijing warlord-controlled government, who had stood aside as the Allies adopted the Treaty of Versailles. Widespread boycotts of Japanese products and strikes against Japanese-owned businesses followed.

Alongside Japan's increasing nationalism, social movements under Taishō Democracy proliferated including promotion of values of universal humanity, including women's liberation, universal suffrage, and equal rights for discriminated classes (*burakumin*). During WWI, Japan had undergone rapid industrialization and urbanization. New factories had sprung up to produce textiles, armaments, ships, and machinery in high demand for export to the Allies and the Central Powers. However, during the industrial buildup, real wages failed to reflect Japan's wartime economic prosperity. Japan's modern labor movement developed out of the resulting dissatisfaction among laborers.

Japan's labor movement began in 1912 with Suzuki Bunji's 鈴木文治 (1885–1946) founding of Friendly Society (*Yūaikai*). At the time, Japanese industrialists and government bureaucrats were suspicious of organized labor. Suzuki believed that cooperation between labor and management was the key to overcoming the suspicion. He developed the Society into a formal labor union movement to achieve this objective.

Socialist and Christian leaders supported the Friendly Society, including political scientist and father of Taishō Democracy Yoshino Sakuzō 吉野作造 (1878-1933); father of the Christian socialist movement Abe Isō 安倍磯雄 (1865-1949); labor activist, social reformer, and Christian pacifist Kagawa Toyohiko 賀川豊彦 (1888-1960); and Quaker agricultural economist and diplomat Nitobe Inazō 新渡戸稲造 (1862-1933). Hongō Church, led by Dōshisha University graduate and disciple of Niijima Jō, Pastor Ebina Danjō 海老名弾正 (1856-1937), published and distributed the journal *New Man* (*Shinjin*). Yoshino, Abe, and Suzuki all contributed articles.

Inspired by the success of the 1917 Russian Revolution, in 1919, Suzuki declared his conversion to socialism. Subsequently, the Friendly Society changed its name to Friendly Society Greater Japan General Federation of Labor to reflect its renewed commitment to the labor movement. The same year, Friendly Society sponsored rallies supporting universal suffrage, the legalization of labor unions, and against the Public Order and Peace Law of 1900 that explicitly targeted Japan's organized labor movements. The 1900 law had imposed restrictions on freedom of speech, assembly, and association. In addition, it outlawed organized labor movements and strikes of any kind.

The Friendly Society's network of activists included several people connected with Niijima Jō and Dōshisha University. Niijima believed that the responsibility to save Japan lay with Christian leaders educated at Dōshisha University. He had faith that Christian education could save the souls of the Japanese people and the nation from the moral and social stagnation of the Japanese state. Furthermore, he believed in challenging the state's moral authority by cultivating independent moral conscience as a weapon for social reform.

Under Niijima's influence, Dōshisha promoted the virtues of benevolence, refusal of adherence to the social bonds of class and family, and the social responsibility of aristocrats. Steeped in the values of Western Puritan individualism, the New England-educated missionary faculty members provided students with rigid training in self-directed non-conformity. They taught students to practice active unwillingness to conform to tradition, including abstaining from tobacco and alcohol and adhering to strict sexual morality. Much like Lu Xun and other May Fourth writers, Japanese Christian converts, including Niijima Jō and many Dōshisha University-educated men who became leaders of Japanese society, shared a mission to save the soul of their country through spiritual transformation.

To promote Japan's spiritual transformation, in 1920, the Shanghai Japanese YMCA began plans to hold its first annual Summer Lecture Series. The lecture series was the organization's first such event. The organizers, including Uchiyama, were in uncharted territory. Uchiyama was active in booking venues, selling several hundred tickets, and hosting visiting speakers. Uchiyama was also responsible for selecting and visiting speakers. Through the Dōshisha connection, Uchiyama knew Suzuki Bunji of the Friendly Society. Suzuki introduced Uchiyama to Yoshino Sakuzō, a political history and theory professor in the Faculty of

Law at Tokyo Imperial University. It was Yoshino who advised Uchiyama on speakers for the lecture series.

Between 1906 and 1909, Yoshino taught law and government at Beiyang College of Law and Politics in Tianjin. Then, through his Tokyo YMCA connections, he developed close ties with Chinese and Korean students in Japan. Shortly after the May Fourth demonstrations, Yoshino published a piece in the *Beijing Morning Post*. In the article, he distinguished "ordinary Japanese" from the ruling military clique. The latter, he argued, could not comprehend the nationalistic sentiments of Chinese youth that inspired the May Fourth Movement. Yoshino assured Chinese readers that ordinary Japanese youth understood the spirit of the Chinese youth. He urged universities of the two countries to initiate faculty exchanges to provide opportunities for discussion of mutual feelings and promote non-governmental cooperation between the two countries.[11]

Working with Yoshino, Uchiyama selected three professors from Japanese universities, each of whom would lecture in Shanghai for one week: Kagawa Toyohiko, pioneer of modern Japanese economics, Fukuda Tokuzō 福田徳三 (1874–1930), and Uchigasaki Sakusaburō 内ヶ崎作三郎 (1877-1947). Each of the three had been associated with or sympathetic to Korean, Taiwanese, and Chinese exchange students in Japan and would appeal to Chinese youth.

Yoshino and Kagawa Toyohiko knew each other through the Friendly Society. On return to Japan in 1917 from his study in the USA, Kagawa was among several intellectuals who joined the Society during WWI. He promoted political activism among workers in Western Japan and built the labor movement in and around the city of Kobe. In the early 1910s, he lived amongst Kobe slum dwellers and realized the limits of philanthropy and temporary relief work. In 1916 while in the USA, Kagawa witnessed 60,000 workers demonstrating in New York City. This experience led him to believe in the importance of organized demonstrations.

Kagawa's trip to participate in the 1920 Shanghai Japanese YMCA Summer Lecture Series was his first to China. During his stay, Uchiyama introduced him to Sun Yat-sen. Inspired by Sun, Kagawa began looking beyond social problems and labor unions to question the role of colonialism. Consequently, he became intensely aware of the tragedies striking Chinese and Korean peoples.

Fukuda Tokuzō and Yoshino founded the Society for Enlightenment (Reimeikai) in late 1918. Comprised of students and other academics, Reimeikai promoted democracy by sponsoring public lectures. Chinese who had studied in Japan knew Fukuda's works well. For example, Uchiyama's customer, radical thinker, and later co-founder of the CPC, Li Dazhao 李大釗, studied Fukuda's work under Yoshino in Tokyo. In a series titled "My Views on Marxism," published between 1919 and 1920, Li introduced Fukuda's writings in Shanghai. At Uchiyama Bookstore, the works of Marxist economist Kawakami Hajime 河上肇 (1879-1946) and Fukuda were among the most popular.

The third speaker Uchigasaki Sakusaburō was a politician, a pastor of the Unitarian Church, a professor at Waseda University, and with Yoshiko Sakuzō and Suzuki Bunji, led the Taishō democracy movement.

Uchiyama traveled to Tokyo in advance to meet face to face with each of the three lecture series participants. In his autobiography, Uchiyama recalls feeling driven to make the lecture series a success and the pure joy he found in organizing it. Perhaps his great enthusiasm for the lecture series derived from discovering his ability as an organizer and liaison. Shanghai Japanese YMCA's Summer Lectures attracted an audience of

Japanese, but more importantly, it attracted many Chinese. Uchiyama's active role in organizing and promoting the 1920 series contributed to the bookstore's transition from a Christian bookstore to one that increasingly catered to Chinese customers.

On May 1, 1924, Maeda Toraji 前田寅治 (1875-1935), a Congregational Church of Japan pastor with Shanghai YMCA, asked Uchiyama to show two visitors from Japan around Shanghai. Labor activists Matsuoka Komakichi 松岡駒吉 (1888-1958) and Nishio Suehiro 西尾末広 (1891-1981) were on the way to Geneva to meet Suzuki Bunji and attend the International Labor Conference. On the way there, they stopped for a few days in Shanghai.

Uchiyama took the Japanese visitors to Shanghai's first May Day International Workers' Day celebration. There he introduced them to the event sponsors, Wang Jingwei 汪精衛 (1893-1944) and Shi Cuntong 施存統 (1899-1970). Wang was a prominent figure in Sun Yat-sen's government, and Shi Cuntong was a principal founder of the Shanghai Marxist Study Group. Later, Wang was known for his involvement in China's collaborationist government and Shi for his active role in the CPC. At the time, both men were Uchiyama Bookstore customers. Wang and Shi invited Suzuki to make the opening speech. Suzuki began his speech, "My Chinese brothers." It was a defining moment in Japanese Chinese relations—amid China's anti-Japanese movement, a moment in which an audience of Chinese people received a Japanese individual with excitement.[12]

Uchiyama's part in the first Shanghai Japanese YMCA Summer Lecture Series and the May Day celebration demonstrates the role he would increasingly play as a mediator—sometimes between unusual combinations of players—when antagonism between Japan and China was high.

Among early customers to Uchiyama's makeshift Christian

bookstore, several held high-ranking positions in Japanese companies. They had formed close friendships with Uchiyama through Shanghai Japanese YMCA and Shanghai Japanese Church. For example, Tsukamoto Suketarō 塚本助太郎 (1900-?) worked for Shanghai Toyota Textile Mill, and Murata Masasuke 村田正亮 (1886-?) served as branch manager at several Mitsui Bussan offices in China. Ibukiyama Tokuji 伊吹山徳司 (1868-1919) was the son of a prominent merchant family and had studied law at Tokyo Imperial University. Rather than becoming a government official, the usual career path for someone of his privileged background, Ibukiyama chose a career where he could contribute to the development of Japanese business. He was Shanghai branch manager for Nippon Yūsen Kabushiki Kaisha (NYK), a major Japanese merchant shipping company. As elite customers such as these men requested specific book titles and advised against others, Uchiyama began to expand his stock beyond Christian-related books.

Following the 1919 Shanghai Japanese YMCA Summer Lecture Series, Chinese who had studied in Japan began visiting the bookshop. Many had spent five to twelve years there and were fluent in Japanese. Like Uchiyama's initial elite Japanese businessmen-customers, they too made particular requests. Following customer suggestions, Uchiyama continued to increase his stock for the general reader, ordering books from suppliers in Tokyo: books in Japanese from Iwanami[13] and books in English from Maruzen.[14]

Customers eagerly awaited the arrival of newly published books. A skilled salesman, around 1919, Uchiyama began posting hand-calligraphed lists of new arrivals at the entrance to Weishengli at Lane 1881, North Sichuan Road. Rather than simply "New Books List," Uchiyama titled his list "Letter of Temptation." To describe new books on offer, he invented catchphrases—"luxury books," "new books," or mysterious phrases such as "fountain of knowledge" or "motivator of faith."

As the bookstore became increasingly busy, the Uchiyamas brought on employees to help Miki. At the same time, Kanzō continued to work for Santendō. Wang Horian, whose cousin worked with Uchiyama at Santendō, was a young migrant to Shanghai from nearby Ningbo in Zhejiang Province. Wang opened the store, helped customers during the day, delivered books, cleaned, and closed. Each morning, an employee named Song prepared the tea utensils. An iron pot of hot water always stood ready on the hibachi. The living room, which doubled as the bookstore, was furnished with a table and four chairs.

By the early 1920s, Uchiyama decided to expand the store and began stockpiling books. The Great Kantō Earthquake of 1923 devastated Tokyo and disrupted the supply chain between Japan and Shanghai but brought expansion and success to Uchiyama Bookstore. Other Shanghai businesses dealing in books from Japan suffered when books from Japan became scarce. In contrast, Uchiyama was able to operate as usual due to his abundant stock.

In 1924, Uchiyama bought the house across the lane from his home-based bookstore. Mirroring Kishida Ginkō's Rakuzendō pharmacy/bookstore in 1880s Shanghai, he moved the bookstore and his Shanghai-based Santendō pharmacy into the new space. Uchiyama equipped the all-white interior with eleven horizontal shelves and eighteen vertical stacks with 198 shelves filled with newly published books. Uchiyama entrusted Wang with recruiting employees, all of whom he recruited from his hometown of Ningbo. The new bookstore continued to serve tea to customers. In the larger space, customers could comfortably sit and chat with each other and with Uchiyama.

Between 1896 and 1937, the Chinese government sent 300,000 students to Japan on scholarship, expecting they would return home with practical skills to modernize China. Instead, many returned with intellectual biases and literary tastes informed by their experiences in Japan. Some fell under the spell of 19th- and 20th-century Western literature and pursued the path of literati (*wenren*). Others, exposed to socialism and Marxism, returned to China as radical advocates of socialism and Marxism.

As soon as new titles in Japanese and English came off the press in Japan, Uchiyama added them to his stock. In China, left-wing materials first published in Japan were almost exclusively available at Uchiyama Bookstore. Bookstore patron and anti-establishment poet Kaneko Mitsuharu 金子光晴 (1895-1975) asserted that Japanese translations of *Das Kapital* and numerous other works on socialist thought poured into Chinese society from the bookshelves of Uchiyama Bookstore and became "the blood and body of revolutionaries."[15]

The customer base grew by word of mouth in the Chinese intellectual community. Customers brought their friends. Their friends became customers and, in turn, brought their friends. In his memoir Uchiyama recalls:

> One day as I was returning from outside, Tian Han introduced me to a few Chinese customers. (He) introduced me one by one to each of them. Tian Han and I chatted incessantly while the others looked at the books with great enthusiasm. Those who arrived at my bookstore for the first time with somebody who can read Japanese also pick up a book because they can read the title. When they look inside, they can read some words and some words they cannot. It is not an overstatement to say that those who pick up a Japanese book once will always learn the Japanese language. In this way, they all became my customers.

They all drank tea, ate some snacks, and went home with various types of books.[16]

This passage reflects the attraction of Japanese books to Chinese intellectuals and activists. Indeed, books in Japanese were so attractive that Chinese who could not read Japanese were inspired to learn the language. As poet and painter Kaneko observed, Uchiyama Bookstore was the "nipple from which Chinese literati acquired their nutrient—namely, knowledge."[17] Hence, it is not surprising that Chinese people grew to comprise two-thirds of the bookstore's customer base.

Late in 1921, Guo Moruo and a group of fellow Chinese students in Japan formed the Creation Society 創造社.[18] Society members soon returned to Beijing and, on May 1, 1922, began publishing *Creation Quarterly* literary magazine 創造季刊. The magazine's content exemplified the "new vernacular literature" with its freedom of form, self-reference, and emphasis on romanticism rather than social responsibility. Creation Society founding members and *Creation Quarterly* contributors Guo, Yu, and Zhang joined the tide of Beijing intellectuals migrating to Shanghai. Soon all three were Uchiyama Bookstore customers.

While the three young Creationists studied in Japan, the late Taishō period's leading novelists, Satō Haruo (1882-1964), Tanizaki Junichirō (1886-1965), and Mushakōji Saneatsu (1885-1976) of the White Birch Society (Shirakaba), were active. Thus, the Creation Society founders shared much in common with these prominent writers. Later, these celebrated Japanese writers would visit Shanghai and connect with Uchiyama at the bookstore. Ever the facilitator of connections, Uchiyama introduced all three Creationists to the Japanese writers whose work inspired *Creation Quarterly*.

Literature of Japan's White Birch Society was particularly

alluring to Creation Society members and others who had returned from studying in Japan. The White Birch Society came together in 1910 around elite alumni of Tokyo's prestigious Gakushūin Peer's School. The Society was a loose association of writers, artists, literary critics, and others who rejected the structures of traditional Japanese literary and artistic styles. Instead, the group embraced idealism, humanism, and individualism over the naturalism that was the dominant trend in literature of the Taishō period. In addition, the works of Leo Tolstoy influenced Shirakaba intellectuals, especially Mushakōji Saneatsu, whose mission was the "creation of non-violent communities."

In 1918, Mushakōji launched the New Village Movement[19] to experiment with communal living based on humanitarian and egalitarian ideals. May Fourth writers regarded the New Village Movement as a model for socialism in practice. In 1919, Zhou Zuoren 周作人, a key figure in the May Fourth Movement and the older of Lu Xun's two younger brothers, introduced the New Village Movement to audiences in China through lectures and publications in *New Youth*. Guo Moruo, dramatist and writer, Tian Han 田漢, Chen Duxiu, and Li Dazhao also embraced the New Village Movement.

Uchiyama Bookstore was a magnet for returned students from Japan who sought access to the latest Marxist literature coming out in Japanese, including Li Dazhao and Chen Duxiu. In the late 1900s, before continuing his studies in Japan, Li had attended Beiyang College of Law and Politics in Tianjin, where he had been a student of Yoshino Sakuzō. After returning to China from Japan, Li became head of the library at Beijing University. A couple of years later, he became a professor of politics, history, and economics there. After attending the 1920 Shanghai Japanese YMCA Summer Lecture Series, Li was among the Chinese who became a customer of Uchiyama Bookstore. Yet, until a journalist friend alerted him, Uchiyama did not realize that his customer was Li Dazhao, a prominent professor from Beijing University. Uchiyama recalled that Li spoke little while purchasing books but commented:

> I like the policy of this bookstore. If the world had a policy like yours, it would move positively. Would you please bring in lots of good books? We will make sure that we don't fall behind by studying these.[20]

Uchiyama believed that wealth comes out of society. Therefore, rather than retaining wealth, individuals should invest in society. In the *mandan* titled "Fertilizer and Footprints," Uchiyama writes that one of his dreams is to "leave our footprints behind in Shanghai."[21] He observed that Japanese people in business have successfully built numerous large textile factories. Yet in terms of fertilizing Shanghai, they have done little or nothing."[22] Uchiyama Kanzō and Miki left behind large footprints in China through Uchiyama Bookstore and Uchiyama Kanzō's work as an organizer, facilitator, and liaison between Chinese and Japanese people.

Endnotes:
1 Akira Iriye, *Cultural Internationalism and World Order* (Baltimore: The John Hopkins University Press, 1997), 14.
2 Leo Ou-fan Lee, *Lu Xun and His Legacy* (Berkeley: University of California Press, 1985), 4.
3 Merle Goldman, ed. *Modern Chinese Literature in the May Fourth Era* (Cambridge: Harvard University Press, 1977), 5.
4 Miwa Kimitada, "Pan-Asianism in Modern Japan: Nationalism, Regionalism and Universalism," in *Pan-Asianism in Modern Japanese History Colonialism, Regionalism and Borders*, eds. Sven Saaler and J. Victor Koschmann (Routledge, 2007), 21-33.
5 Kentarō Kaneko, "A 'Japanese Monroe Doctrine' and Manchuria," *Contemporary Japan*, 1 (1932), 176-184. Kaneko recounts his days and conversations as Roosevelt's guest during the negotiations over the Treaty of Portsmouth ending the Russo-Japanese War.
6 George H. Blakeslee. "The Japanese Monroe Doctrine," *Foreign Affairs*, July 1933. https://www.foreignaffairs.com/print/node/1111508.
7 Erez Manela, *The Wilsonian Moment: Self-Determination and the International Origins of Anticolonial Nationalism* (Oxford: Oxford University Press, 2007), 62.
8 Margaret MacMillan, *Paris 1919: Six Months That Changed the World*. (Random House: 2003), 318.
9 Naoko Shimazu, *Japan, Race and Equality*. (Routledge 1998), 114.
10 Shimazu, *Japan, Race and Equality*, 115.
11 Zhang, Henpu, "Yoshino hakase hōmonki: Yoshino Sakuzō kenkyū ni okeru chūgoku shiryō katsuyō no ichirei," *Seiji kenkyū* 56 (2009), 129.
12 Koizumi Yuzuru, *Rojin to Uchiyama Kanzō*, (Tokyo: Kōdansha, 1979), 119.
13 Iwanami Bookstore and Publisher, founded 1913 in Tokyo by

Iwanami Shigeo, was a pioneer in offering literature and science titles for the public. It is known for scholarly publications, editions of classical Japanese literature, and dictionaries. In Shanghai, Uchiyama followed in Iwanami Shoten's footsteps by selling and publishing books. Iwanami's flagship store continues to operate in Tokyo's Jinbōchō district.

14 Maruzen Bookstore and Publisher is one of Japan's leading booksellers. Founded in 1869, in Yokohama, it was Japan's first joint-stock company. Fukuzawa Yukichi, one of Japan's foremost intellectuals and educators and a leader in introducing Western culture to Japan, recommended that Hayashi Yūteki found the store. Maruzen imported Western publications and other goods and made information about overseas cultures available to Japanese customers. In 1870 its flagship store opened in Tokyo's Nihonbashi district, where it still operates today.

15 Kaneko Mitsuharu, *Dokurohai* (Tokyo: Chūō Kōronsha, 2004).

16 Takatsuna Hirofumi, "Kokusai toshi" shanhai no naka no nihonjin, (Tokyo: Kenbun Shuppan, 2009), 204.

17 Kaneko Mitsuharu, *Dokurohai*, 160-161.

18 Yu Dafu 郁達夫 (1896-1945), Zhang Ziping 張資平 (1893-1959) and others.

19 New Village Movement (Atarashiki-mura) was a Japanese utopian movement founded in 1918 by author and artist Mushakōji Saneatsu. The Movement aimed to build a socialist community where people from different backgrounds could live together in an egalitarian, nurturing environment based on mutual aid and shared manual labor. The Movement espoused peaceful resolution of conflict rather than revolution. In Republican Period China, the Movement emphasized the development of national consciousness through manual work and the experience of country life and connection with rural

people and the village as sources of knowledge.
20 Uchiyama Kanzō, *Rojin no omoide*, (Tokyo: Shakai Shisōsha, 1979), 285.
21 Uchiyama Kanzō, *Shanhai ringo* (Tokyo: Kōdansha, 1942), 178.
22 Uchiyama Kanzō, *Rojin no omoide*, 285.

FOURTH TURN OF THE KALEIDOSCOPE

A SINO-JAPANESE CULTURAL SALON (1926-1930)

THERE WAS A trend of copious magazine reading among Shanghai's Japanese community during this period. Some families subscribed to as many as ten magazines per month. In the late 1920s, Hasegawa Saburō, who knew Uchiyama from Shanghai Japanese Church, began operating a magazine section next to Uchiyama Bookstore in Weishengli, offering magazines for adults and children. Later the magazine section moved close to Fumin Hospital on North Sichuan Road. Another magazine branch opened on Wusong Road.[1]

The train line running along North Sichuan Road from downtown Shanghai extended north beyond the boundary of the International Settlement ending at the intersection of North Sichuan Road and Shanyin Road. In addition, Japanese investment companies were building new lane house developments for the growing number of Japanese working in Shanghai. Therefore, to accommodate the continued growth of the bookstore and respond to an increasing market in the area for Japanese materials, in 1929, Uchiyama Bookstore moved to 2048 North Sichuan Road at the intersection with Shanyin Road. This remained the bookstore's flagship location until the local Chinese government authorities requisitioned it on October 23, 1945.

The first floor was devoted to sales. The second floor was a flexible space where customers chatted over tea, Uchiyama entertained his visitors from Japan, and groups like the Chinese Drama Research Society (Shinageki Kenkyūkai) held their meetings. When the bookstore moved from Weishengli to North Sichuan Road, the Uchiyamas moved into a lane house behind the bookstore in Qianaili (千愛里).[2] The Japanese overseas investment company Tōakōgyō built Qianaili in 1922. Typical of the better Shanghai residential developments of the 1920s, it was equipped with modern conveniences — running water, electricity, and gas.

Before the Uchiyamas relocated the bookstore from Weishengli to North Sichuan Road, it had already become popular among Shanghai's Chinese and Japanese intellectual communities. It was the center of Uchiyama's extensive activities as a cultural liaison between Chinese and Japanese intellectuals in both countries. Furthermore, since 1925, the bookstore had been the venue of Uchiyama's Sino-Japanese salon — Mandankai. The bookstore was also well-known among Chinese students who had studied in Japan, Japanese visitors to Shanghai, and Japanese residents of Shanghai. They gathered at the bookstore to discuss wide-ranging topics of mutual interest.

From the mid to late-1920s, Uchiyama Bookstore and its salon grew in size and popularity with customers. The growth occurred within the context of multiple interconnected factors that emerged and intersected in 1920s Shanghai: the arrival of May Fourth writers from Beijing; a vibrant book culture that greatly expanded Chinese intellectuals' access to new ideas; the relative ease with which educated Chinese could become literate in Japanese; extraterritoriality of Shanghai's international concession settlements; and convenience of travel between Japan and Shanghai.

A growing number of bookshops, translation services, and publishers contributed to the expansion of Shanghai's book culture. Publishers ranged from a few large organizations established in the early 20th century to small-scale, independently run publishing houses, some of which had been operating for years. For example, Kishida Ginkō's Shanghai Rakuzendō branch opened in 1880 on Henan Middle Road in the International Settlement (Chapter 2). Nihondō, established in 1906, was among Shanghai's first Japanese bookstores. It published Japanese language maps and books on Chinese topics, especially travel-related books. Nihondō also carried magazines and was the Shanghai distributor for Japanese language newspapers *Hōchi* and *Tōkyō mainichi* (*Tokyo Daily News*). Shiseidō, established in 1913, was another of Shanghai's early Japanese bookstores. It carried numerous Japanese-language newspapers from publishers in both Japan and Shanghai. When the Uchiyamas opened their bookstore in 1917, selling Bibles and Christian-related titles out of their home, Uchiyama Bookstore joined the ranks of Shanghai's Japanese bookstores.

During the 1920s and 1930s, Fuzhou Road, known to the present as Shanghai's bookshop street, became the center of the city's publishing sector. Two major publishing houses, Commercial Press and Zhonghua Press, both on Fuzhou Road, dominated the market. They specialized in textbooks and translated and published other works, including book series and journals. Alongside these long-established publishers, small-scale independent publishers and bookstores sprung up—eighteen during 1928 alone, the apex of new publishing in Shanghai. Kaiming Press, established in 1926 to promote "new" literature, was one such press. Well before its launch, Kaiming founders, a group of May Fourth intellectuals including realist novelist Mao Dun 茅盾 (1896-1981) and Ye Shengtao 葉聖陶 (1894-1988), were all customers of Uchiyama Bookstore.[3] Kaiming launched the literary careers of several of its founders and other young writers. There were also second-hand bookstores, English-language bookstores, such as Kelly & Walsh, the Chinese American Publishing Company, which published and imported books, and the Zeitgeist Bookstore, a Comintern-funded outlet for communist materials. Many of these shops clustered in the streets around Fuzhou Road.

Kaiming's first editor, novelist and translator Zhao Jingshen 趙景深 (1902-1985), recalls that part of every writer's daily routine was making rounds of Shanghai bookstores. In 1929, on a tour of bookstores from his home in Zhabei, Zhao set off on Baoxing Road, first downtown, then back to Zhabei on North Sichuan Road. Along the way, Zhao counted forty-eight bookstores. He noted that some were owned and operated by Chinese and others by British, Americans, or Japanese.

> My house was in Zhabei,[4] and I frequently went to the station by rickshaw, then by tram on Sixth Road to No. 5 Horse Road (Guangdong Road near Fuzhou Road) to take a peek at the bookstores to find new books. Oops, my legs move on their own accord. First to Yadong, then turn south to Zhenshanmei, and from Zhenshanmei, go straight to the long-established bookstores of

Minzhi, Commercial Press, and Zhonghua. Westward from Zhonghua is the bookstore town of Fuzhou Road, where bookstores crowd together. Turning toward the north is the newspaper street with two bookstores, Xinyue and Kaiming. I wonder how many there are in total—eighteen bookstores?[5]

Translations from Western languages into Japanese made new knowledge increasingly accessible to the Chinese intellectual community and contributed to Shanghai's flourishing book culture. In 1926 Tanizaki Junichirō commented, "most new knowledge that Chinese acquire is through Japanese sources, including Japanese translations of Western books. There are Western bookstores, though, unfortunately, the selection of titles they stock in original languages is limited. Like other Shanghai bookstores, they must order English language titles from Tokyo's Maruzen Bookstore."[6]

In December 1926, Japanese publisher Kaizōsha[7] began offering a 63-volume series of Japanese language literature priced at one *yen* per book. Other publishers quickly followed suit, kicking off the "one-yen book (*enpon*) boom." Soon, a wide variety of books, many translated into Japanese from Western languages, became readily accessible and affordable to the Japanese public and patrons of Shanghai booksellers who imported the titles from Tokyo. The following year, Uchiyama ordered multiple sets of Kaizōsha's Japanese language "Complete Works" collections: *Complete Works of Japanese Literature* (1,000 sets), *Complete Works of World Literature* (1,000 sets), *Complete Works of Marx and Engels* (400 sets), *Complete Works of New Economics* (200 sets), and *Complete Works of Law* (200 sets).

While studying in Japan, some Chinese students turned from economics and medicine to literature and emerged as the

May Fourth Movement writers. These included playwright screenwriter, CPC member Xia Yan 夏衍 (1900-1995), Zhou Shuren (Lu Xun), and his younger brother Zhou Zhouren. Returning to China in the 1920s and 1930s, these men and other Chinese literati supplemented their incomes from writing by translating Western works from Japanese into Chinese. Books from Uchiyama's abundant stock of Japanese literature served as sources from which writers produced their Chinese translations. Between 1919 and 1937, Chinese writers who had studied in Japan translated more than 120 Japanese titles into Chinese, including modern Japanese drama, poetry, literary criticism, short stories, novels, and nonfiction works on law, politics, and education. Additionally, between 1919 and 1945, Chinese periodicals carried translations of over three hundred Japanese literary works.

Because Chinese characters are the source of Japanese *kanji*, learning to read Japanese is relatively easy for educated Chinese. Tanizaki Junichirō noted:

> The Japanese language is difficult to speak, but learning Japanese is much easier than learning European languages for Chinese people. It may take a few years for Chinese learners to appreciate novels or plays, but half a year can suffice to understand books on law or science. That is why Chinese who are eager to absorb new knowledge compete to learn Japanese.[8]

Thus, teaching Japanese to Chinese presented another opportunity for those who had studied in Japan to supplement their income. Feng Zikai 豐子愷 (1898-1975), a prolific artist, writer, and intellectual influential in music, art, literature, philosophy, and translation, founded Lida Academy in 1925 to teach Japanese. Lida was renowned for its teachers. Besides Feng, teachers included Mao Dun, Ye Shengtao, and scholar and educator Chen Wangdao 陳望道 (1891-1977). Later Chen was the first to translate the Communist Manifesto into Chinese. Journalist Huang Yuan 黃源 (1905-2003) and Kaiming's Xia Mianzun 夏丏尊 (1886-1946) were among the many who studied Japanese at Lida.

Western works contained words for which there were no Japanese translations. Therefore, Japanese translators created new words by imitating the sounds of the foreign words using Japanized Chinese. Although there were dictionaries to assist readers in understanding the meaning of such transliterations, they were inaccurate. In 1929 Zheng Boqi 鄭伯奇 (1895-1979), film writer, novelist, literary theorist, Creation Society member, and pioneer of the left-wing literary movement, approached Uchiyama with a proposal for a Japanese language school. Zheng asserted, "we need textbooks and schools to teach proper Japanese; otherwise, we will have an unknown language."[9] Uchiyama recognized that a Japanese language school would expand his market in the Chinese intellectual community and proposed that the bookstore provide the facility and that Zheng run the language school. Through a good friend who supported the idea, Uchiyama quickly secured free use of the second floor of the Shanghai Purchasing Department on Liyang Road.

Uchiyama and Zheng recruited students for the school, Uchiyama through the bookstore, and Zheng through his notoriety among Chinese students. The classes attracted more and more students, two other teachers joined, and the school soon needed extra space. Uchiyama secured two more classrooms on the first floor of the Japanese YMCA. The school expanded further to include rooms at the Jewish School, and the teaching staff expanded to six, including Zheng. Ultimately the school operated five classrooms of thirty students each, and the library held around 5,000 Japanese books. The quality of students was uniformly high and included many university students.

Writers, activists, and other intellectuals were drawn to Shanghai by the city's book culture. Extraterritoriality in the city's foreign concessions was also an attractive feature. Under the extraterritoriality rights,[10] international concession residents were immune from prosecution under Chinese law. Thus, technically each settlement operated under the laws of its mother country. In reality, settlement residents enjoyed immunity from all laws but those of the concession where they lived. Initially, only foreigners involved in either Shanghai-based trade or Christian organizations had the right of residence within the concession boundaries. Chinese nationals were explicitly prohibited.

During the Taiping Rebellion (1850-1864), refugees flooded into the relative safety of Shanghai, overwhelmed the housing supply in the Chinese-controlled sections, spilled over into the foreign concessions, and left foreign authorities with no choice but to allow Chinese people to live within the foreign concession boundaries. Thus, Shanghai's foreign concessions became increasingly multicultural. After 1905 when the Japanese prevailed in the Russo-Japanese War, Shanghai experienced a massive influx of Japanese immigrants seeking business opportunities or simply livelihood in Shanghai. By the 1910s, Japanese nationals accounted for the largest single group of foreigners residing in Shanghai. In 1923 when "red" Bolsheviks prevailed in the Russian civil war over "white" monarchy loyalists, White Russians poured into northern China. Many continued south to Shanghai. In Europe between WWI and WWII, Jews experienced increasing persecution. Many fled from Germany and other European countries. Shanghai's international concessions did not require citizenship documents for entry, and many Jewish refugees arrived.

"Floating populations," including Chinese from other parts of China, Japanese, White Russians, and European Jews, settled in self-contained communities within the French Concession and the International Settlement and in Chinese-controlled areas along extra-settlement roads that extended north beyond the boundary of the International Settlement. The International Settlement operated street lighting, water, and telephone lines running along these major streets, such as North Sichuan Road north of Wujin Road. Though the International Settlement authorities exercised administrative authority over the roads, local Chinese authorities exercised authority over the communities of houses and businesses lining these roads.

In his *mandan* storytelling style Uchiyama described the humorous situations that took place along extra-settlement roads:

> A settlement police officer is running after a thief on North Sichuan Road. The thief manages to run away into a lane. If there are no Chinese police officers in sight, the thief is in luck. He can stop running and stroll along, swinging his arms because the settlement officer cannot come into the lane under the control of the Chinese authorities. Even if the settlement officer were to take one step off the extra-settlement road, it would infringe on China's national sovereignty. The same applies in the opposite situation. What a nuisance this road is![11]

Communities segregated by nationality within various official jurisdictions were part of everyday life in Shanghai. A good example was Rokusankaen 六三花園, a five-acre Japanese garden in "Little Japan" — home to the majority Japanese community within the boundaries of the International Settlement.[12] Rokusankaen, near the south gate of modern Lu Xun Park, was open for free to the Japanese.[13] In contrast, Chinese and Japanese were not allowed to enter Western gardens in the foreign concessions. Within the walls of Rokusankaen, among other structures, was one of Shanghai's most famous high-end Japanese *ryōtei*.[14] Uchiyama described it:

> You enter through the main gate surrounded by high and long walls. You pass through a vast garden filled with beautifully planted trees, and there lies a building shining with lamps like a palace. A beautifully dressed lady leads you upstairs into a large room with new *tatami* mats and golden folding screens. How beautiful! I call this cuisine that feeds the eye.[15]

Japanese entertained business and political guests in Rokusankaen. Sino-Japanese cultural exchanges also took place there. For example, in 1912, the Japanese revolutionary activist Miyazaki Tōten organized a welcoming party for Sun-Yatsen at Rokusankaen. In 1935, Uchiyama arranged a meeting at Rokusankaen to introduce Noguchi Yonejirō 野口米次郎 (1875-1947), an influential writer of poetry, fiction, essays, and literary criticism in both English and Japanese, to the *Asahi* newspaper's Shanghai branch manager and Lu Xun.

Relative to the suppression the May Fourth writers experienced in Beijing, proletarian writers in Shanghai in the late 1920s were relatively free to live, write, and publish with little fear of persecution by the Chinese authorities. Li Liewen 黎烈文 (1904-1972) of the Commercial Press, Xia Mianzun of Kaiming Press, Lu Xun's brothers, Zhou Zuoren and Zhou

Jianren, and Xia Yan all settled in Shanghai after having studied in Japan. Mao Dun and Creation Society members Guo Moruo and Yu Dafu came from Beijing. Lu Xun, who fled Beijing for the south in 1926, arrived in Shanghai in 1927 from Guangzhou, where he had taught at Sun Yat-sen University. All these radical writers became patrons of Uchiyama Bookstore. Several of them, including Lu Xun, lived within easy walking distance of each other and the bookstore.[16]

Before leaving Beijing, Lu Xun had learned from Shimizu Yasuzō 清水安三 (1891-1988), an educator and graduate of Dōshisha University, about Uchiyama and his bookstore. Two days after arriving in Shanghai, Lu Xun made his first visit to the bookstore and, a few days later, conversed for the first time with Uchiyama. When Lu Xun arrived in Shanghai on October 3, 1927, he was already one of China's most famous intellectuals. Lu Xun would reign as the "grand old man" of letters in Shanghai until his death. He would be the scourge of the authorities, patron of radical youth, and at the center of Uchiyama's network of left-wing writers and activists.

On April 12, 1927, a few months before Lu Xun's arrival in Shanghai, forces in Shanghai supporting General Chiang Kai-shek and conservative elements in the KMT had carried out a mass suppression of the CPC and related organizations in Shanghai. For months afterward, the local authorities, sometimes with the cooperation of foreign concession authorities, carried out periodic crackdowns on communists, their sympathizers, and others deemed to be opposed to the KMT. Consequently, upon his arrival in Shanghai, Lu Xun took precautions.

Uchiyama Bookstore began serving as Lu Xun's "post office," to which he directed his mail. He also paid and received all manuscript fees through the bookstore. Everyone knew that, unless he was ill, Lu Xun came to the bookstore every afternoon.

He sat at the back of the store while Uchiyama or an employee sat near the entrance. Those who came to see Lu Xun feigned browsing among books, signaled, and then met Lu Xun behind the bookshelves. Lu Xun had complete trust in Uchiyama:

> I have been frequenting the place for the past three years. It is safer than dealing with some of the Shanghai literati, as Uchiyama is in the business of making money. He is not involved in secret investigations. I am convinced he will not be selling blood.[17]

Under the 1895 Treaty of Shimonoseki, ending the First Sino-Japanese War, Japan had secured trading rights and had joined other foreign powers operating out of Shanghai's International Settlement. As a result, Shanghai was one of the few cities in the world that Japanese nationals could enter without a passport or an identification check. So, Japanese came in ever-increasing numbers, many to do business, others to seek their fortune in the booming city, and others on holiday or school excursions. Ease of entry also made Shanghai an attractive destination for Japanese revolutionaries, radicals, criminals, and others on the run from Japanese authorities.

In 1923, the passage by steamship between Nagasaki and Shanghai, depending on weather and currents, took 24 to 27 hours. With regularly scheduled sailings between the two cities, and in 1920, a second-class ticket for as little as thirty yen, many Nagasaki Japanese called Shanghai home and received letters from Japan addressed, "Nagasaki Prefecture, Shanghai City."

During the 1920s, Shanghai became increasingly cosmopolitan relative to Tokyo, especially after the Great Kantō Earthquake of 1923 destroyed much of the city. World-class cosmopolitan Shanghai attracted Japanese artists and intellectuals who felt increasingly stifled in Tokyo. For these Japanese, Shanghai represented "the other" and was a source of inspiration. Such literary visitors knew Uchiyama Bookstore as "Shanghai Customs." After arriving in Shanghai, through Uchiyama, all such visitors arranged meetings with the Chinese cultural literati. The bookstore's profit was relatively high—around 80,000 yen per month. Hence, Uchiyama could afford to host parties for Sino-Japanese literati—after all, who would refuse fine dining? Various incidents during Tanizaki Junichirō, Kaneko Mitsuharu, and other Japanese proletarian writers' visits to Shanghai reflect Uchiyama's skill as a host and cultural mediator.

Tanizaki Junichirō visited China in 1918, hoping to meet young writers, but he met none due to his lack of connections. So, in January 1926, he tried again. During a welcoming party in Shanghai hosted by Mitsui Bank's Shanghai branch manager, one of the guests told Tanizaki, "Young Chinese artists are beginning a New Culture Movement. They are translating Japanese novels and plays. If you don't believe me, go to Uchiyama Bookstore and find out for yourself." A few days later, Tanizaki dropped by the bookstore and met Uchiyama. He learned that sixty-seven Chinese Tokyo Imperial University alumni worked at Shanghai's Commercial Press by chatting with Uchiyama. Planning for translation and publication of Japanese novels and plays into Chinese, they kept a constant eye on publications coming out of Tokyo.

Uchiyama promptly arranged to host a reception for Tanizaki. At the event, Tanizaki met writer Guo Moruo, dramatist Tian Han, Peking Opera actor and a founder of Chinese spoken drama Ouyang Yuqian, revolutionary realist poet Wang Duqing 王獨清 (1898-1940), oil painter Chen Baoyi 陳抱一 (1893-1945), and linguist-translator Fang Guangtao 方光燾 (1898-1964). The discussion ranged over a wide variety of topics from movies and translation to Japanese drama and literary communities.

In March 1926, anti-establishment poet Kaneko Mitsuharu and his wife arrived in Shanghai for a two-month-long stay. Kaneko carried a letter of introduction from Tanizaki addressed to Guo Moruo, Tian Han, and Uchiyama. In short order, Uchiyama organized and hosted a reception for Kaneko and Tanizaki with Tian Han, Chen Baoyi, Feng Guangtao, Ouyang Yuqian, and others. Kaneko recalled, "Tian spoke with confidence and passion on movie production."[18]

Kaneko revisited Shanghai in 1928, this time staying four months. During this visit, Uchiyama introduced him to Lu Xun. Subsequently, Kaneko and Lu Xun met frequently at the bookstore. During Shanghai's chilly winter months, Kaneko and his wife joined the crowd of friends who gathered at the bookstore to warm up near the stove. In his memoir, Kaneko, recalling the Chinese Song Dynasty novel *Water Margins*, compared the Uchiyama Bookstore to the fortress on Mount Liang in the Liangshan Marsh. He likened those who gathered at Uchiyama Bookstore to the 108 outlaws who gathered on Mount Liang to plan a rebellion against the government.[19]

In April 1927, proletarian writers Komaki Ōmi 小牧近江 (1894-1978) and Satomura Kinzō 里村欣三 (1902-1945) turned up without warning at the bookstore. Komaki was a pioneer in the Japanese Proletarian Literature Movement, an anti-war activist, and a translator. The two had come to Shanghai at the invitation of Henri Barbusse, founder of the Clarté Movement, to represent the Japanese proletarian journal *Bungei sensen* at an international conference organized by the League Against Imperialism.[20]

Japan's Peace Preservation Law amendment of 1925 had explicitly targeted communist sympathizers. Consequently, the Tokkō (military thought control police) was engaged in intensified suppression of communism.[21] Onboard the ship from

KALEIDOSCOPE

Nagasaki, Komaki and Satomura hid from the onboard Tokkō patrol. Disembarking, they posed as members of an EACCA group. Once in Shanghai, they stayed within the relative safety of the French Concession to escape the eye of local Tokkō, local Chinese government authorities, and agents of the Japanese government, all of which were active within the Japanese community of the International Settlement.

Because of the dangerous political climate, organizers canceled the conference. Nonetheless, Komaki and Satomura made good use of their time in China and, thanks to Uchiyama, met several Chinese counterparts:

> We visited Uchiyama Bookstore. The owner was a plump guy with a shaved head. He knows Tanizaki (Junichirō) and Akutagawa (Ryūnosuke). Yu (Dafu) and Tian Han all go to his house. We returned to our lodge after sunset. There we found to our surprise, Yu Dafu's name card on the table![22]

Ultimately, during their time in Shanghai, Komaki and Satomura met some twenty Chinese literati. Subsequently, a group picture, including poet Yu Dafu, Guo Moruo, Wang Duqing, and Creation Society member Cheng Fangwu, ran in an issue of *Bungei sensen*. Alongside the picture, there was a piece of calligraphy by Tian Han, a gift to Komaki and Satomura. It read, "All Proletarian Writers of the World Unite!"

As well as facilitating meetings between Chinese literati and their Japanese counterparts, Uchiyama also opened doors for face-to-face meetings between members of the Chinese literary community who knew each other only through their writings and commentaries. In the late 1920s, the Creation Society was at war with the Literary Research Association over the definition of revolutionary literature. In 1925, Guo Moruo had converted to Marxism and had led the Creation Society onto the path of revolutionary proletariat literature. Lu Xun and his disciples in the Literary Research Association called for literature to promote radical social change. Although Literary Research Association writers and Creation Society writers fiercely debated through their writing on everyday issues, members of one group had not necessarily met counterparts in the other group. Uchiyama's gathering in honor of Tanizaki not only provided a venue for Sino-Japanese cultural engagement but was also an opportunity for estranged Chinese literary figures to meet and converse face-to-face.

In June 1927, Tian Han made a brief visit to Japan. The trip's success was primarily due to Uchiyama. Besides arranging Tian's boat ticket to Nagasaki, Uchiyama arranged for Tian to meet several Japanese writers. Satomura Kinzō, who had met Tian two months earlier in Shanghai through Uchiyama, headed the delegation that welcomed Tian in Tokyo. Outside the train station, novelist and poet Satō Haruo, with whom Tian had maintained a close relationship since studying in Japan, and novelist Muramatsu Shōfū 村松梢風 (1889-1962), who had met Tian in Shanghai through Satō, joined the welcoming party. In addition, Uchiyama's close friend Yamamoto Sanehiko 山本実彦 (1885-1952), of Tokyo's Kaizōsha publishing house, arranged a reception for Tian. During Tian's four days in Tokyo, he met more than thirty Japanese writers. While in Tokyo, Tian invited Satō to visit Shanghai. When Satō arrived in Shanghai two weeks later, Tian, swamped with film industry-related work, called on Creation Society poet and short story writer Yu Dafu to host Satō in his place.

Uchiyama Bookstore served as a link for sharing information and contacts between China and Japan for both Chinese who had studied in Japan and Japanese writers traveling to Shanghai. Because people of both nationalities could freely travel back and forth between Japan and Shanghai, many found opportunities to connect in both countries and formed lasting friendships. Over time as writers in both China and Japan introduced their friends in the other country to each other, the Sino-Japanese literary circle expanded.

Poet Huang Ying 黃瀛 (1906-2005), whose father was Chinese and mother was Japanese, had moved back and forth between China and Japan throughout his early years. He was schooled in Japan, in part as a Chinese exchange student, and in the 1920s lived in Nanjing. Huang knew of Uchiyama Bookstore through his friends, the playwright Tian Han and the modern artist Wang Daoyuan 王道遠 (1892-1965), and had seen Uchiyama's articles in Yamamoto Sanehiko's *Kaizō* magazine. Japanese language books were difficult to find, so he traveled to Shanghai to visit the bookstore about once a month and bought books spanning a broad range of subjects. He and Uchiyama had become close, and on arrival at the bookstore, one of the shop attendants would lead him to a small *tatami* room at the back. Over tea, Uchiyama recounted stories from his past in Japan to Huang. Lu Xun heard from visiting Japanese writers that a Chinese poet named Huang lived in China and wrote poetry in Japanese. Lu Xun asked Uchiyama to arrange a meeting and, around 1929, met Huang. In his memoir, Huang recalls that he and Lu Xun discussed manuscript fees, theater in Japan, and woodblock printing.

Alongside Uchiyama Bookstore's wide selection of books and magazines, Uchiyama hosted an informal cultural salon. The idea for the assemblage, which came to be known as Shanghai Mandankai or simply Mandankai, originated with Tsukamoto Suketarō, a businessman, and Masuya Jisaburō 升屋治三郎 (1894-1974), a critic of theatrical arts. Both men were

Chinese opera aficionados and had organized Shanghai YMCA's Chinese Drama Research Society. Mandankai began with twenty members comprised of Japanese writers and artists and Chinese new culture literati and was a venue for participants to talk among themselves freely. The group met monthly at Uchiyama Bookstore over rice crackers and tea supplied by the Uchiyamas. The lively discussions often lasted until two or three in the morning. There were only three requirements for membership: the desire to engage with fellow artists and literati, passionate interest in the topics, and an invitation from Uchiyama.

Most of the early Mandankai participants had studied in Japan. These included playwright Zheng Boqi, dramatist Ouyang Yuqian, translator and historian of Japanese literature Xie Liuyi 謝六逸 (1898-1945), poets Tian Han and Wang Duqing, Creation Society members Yu Dafu, Guo Moruo, Tao Jingsun 陶晶孫 (1897-1952), and Peking Opera artist Mei Langfang 梅蘭芳 (1894-1961). In addition to its founders Tsukamoto and Masuya, early members were Maeda Toraji of the Shanghai Japanese YMCA, literary critic Takeuchi Yoshio 竹内良夫 (1916-1993), and others in government-related roles or corporate-level positions in textiles, banking, and transportation sectors for whom the arts and literature were a hobby. Medical doctor Ishii Masayoshi was one such member. He was known among members as Doctor Goethe because of his passion for the works of Goethe. Chinese expert in the ministry of Foreign Affairs Shimizu Tōzō 清水董三 (1893-1970) was another such member. He was an avid calligrapher and professor of the Chinese language at EACCA. Uchiyama Bookstore published his books and essays. Japanese journalists also joined the group and included translator and EACCA graduate Yamaguchi Shinichi 山口慎一 (1907-1980).

Between 1927 and 1930, Uchiyama Bookstore published Mandankai's magazine *Kaleidoscope* (*La Kalejdoskope*). Any member who paid a minimal monthly fee could contribute one page to each issue in either Chinese or Japanese. For example, Zheng Boqi contributed a piece about the Shanghai Art and Drama Society. Yamaguchi and Masuya wrote about film as a more effective medium than literature for communicating with the masses. Essays contributed by Creation Society members signaled the growing influence of left-wing literature. There was even a piece by Uchiyama Kanzō published under his Chinese name Wu Qishan 鄔其山.[23] Although the articles were of mixed quality, the magazine signaled that Uchiyama had won the trust of Chinese students who had studied in Japan and that the group dynamic he nurtured among the bookstore's Chinese and Japanese patrons was positive.[24]

Though Uchiyama Bookstore is known for its monthly Mandankai, the bookstore was also well known for the informal chatting that invariably took place there. The bookstore was an ideal place to take a break. There was always tea and occasionally snacks. There was a fire in the stove during the winter with people gathered around to warm up and chat. Bookstore regular Doctor Okuda observed:

> There are chatting sessions going on almost every day at the bookstore, from morning to evening. It is not as if it begins with somebody or at a particular time, but with Uchiyama's greeting, "Welcome! Come and sit." One by one, people gather. Meanwhile, Miki brings tea. Sooner or later, most world problems would come up for discussion at one of these sessions.[25]

Okuda recounted a conversation between calligrapher Kojima Shizuko 児島静子 (1915-2004) and Lu Xun. Kojima asked Lu Xun how he thought Sino-Japanese relations would develop.

Lu Xun asserted that the relationship would deteriorate. "The negotiations are going to worsen too. I don't know what Japan is thinking. Neither do I know what China is thinking. When those who don't know what they're doing talk to each other, it is the most dangerous."²⁶ Others interjected their views. Discussion took off.

Experimental modernist writer Yokomitsu Riichi 横光利一 (1898-1947) described the informal discussions as "more interesting than walking around Shanghai" and risked missing his return voyages to Japan by delaying his departure from the bookstore for the quay until the last minute.

Yu Dafu was known for his comment on the role Uchiyama and the Uchiyama Bookstore played in 1920s Shanghai and, by extension, in China: "It is not the Japanese military that is occupying China. It is Uchiyama Bookstore".²⁷

KALEIDOSCOPE

Endnotes:

1 Takatsuna Hirofumi,"*Kokusai toshi*" *shanhai no naka no nihonjin*, 216.
2 Qianaili, No. 3, Lane 2, Shanyin Road, 千愛里, 山陰路2弄3號.
3 Other founders were Xia Mianzun (1886-1946), Zhang Xichen (1889-1969), and Zheng Zhenduo (1898-1958).
4 Zhabei was in a Chinese-controlled section of Shanghai. The former Zhabei district is now part of Jian'an district.
5 Leo Ou-fan Lee. *Shanghai Modern: the Flowering of a New Urban Culture in China, 1930-1945*. Cambridge: Harvard University Press, 1999. (p.121)
6 Ozaki, *Shanhai 1930-nen*, (Tokyo: Iwanami Shinsho, 1989), 31.
7 Kaizōsha was established during the Taishō period. In 1919 after the end of WWI, the company began publishing Kaizō (Reorganize/Restructure/Reconstruct). Although well known for carrying works of fiction, its socialist and communist articles about labor and social problems appealed to readers. The editor Yamamoto Sanehiko was a life-long friend of Uchiyama and had a keen interest in China. In July 1926, with the help of Uchiyama, he launched a "China Special" edition to which Guo Moruo, Liang Qichao, and Hu Shi contributed articles. Though Kaizōsha is no longer in the publishing business, the company operates a chain of bookstores in the Tokyo area's Narita and Haneda International Airports.
8 Tanizaki Junichirō, *Shanhai kōyūki* ed. Chiba Shunji. (Tokyo: Misuzu Shobō, 2004), 565.
9 Uchiyama Kanzō, *Sonhē ōhe: Shanhai seikatsu sanjūgonen*, (Tokyo: Iwanami Shinsho, 1949), 53.
10 The British Settlement was established in 1845 and the French Concession in 1849. In 1863 the British and Americans formed a joint settlement known as the International Settlement. Subsequently other foreign powers, including Japan, won

equivalent concession rights and joined the International Settlement. The French Concession was under the direction of the French Consul-General. The International Settlement operated under the management of the Shanghai Municipal Council comprised of elected foreign ratepayers, mainly British. Each of them controlled substantial properties in the settlement.

11 Maruyama Noboru, *Shanhai monogatari: Kokusai toshi shanhai to nitchū bunkajin*, (Tokyo: Kōdansha Gakujutsu Bunko, 2004), 27.
12 Christian Henriot, "Little Japan in Shanghai: An Insulated Community, 1875-1945" in *New Frontiers: Imperialism's New Communities in East Asia*, 1842-1945, eds., Robert Bikers and Christian Henriot (Manchester University Press, 2012), 146-169.
13 Rokusankaen (Rokusan Garden) was built in 1907 on West Jiangwan Road near the corner of Huayuan Road (so named because it ran alongside the garden) 西江灣路 240弄 at 花園路. The ryōtei, along with other structures, was within the walls of the garden. The ryōtei's predecessor was a simple noodle shop opened on Boone Road (now Tangu Road) by Nagasaki native Rokusaburō Shiraishi to serve others from Nagasaki, and originally named Rokusanan 六三庵 (Rokusan Cottage) reflecting his first name Rokusaburō. As noodle shop's business expanded, he changed the name to Rokusantei 六三亭 (Rokusan Pavilion), bought property further north, and built Rokusankaen including the ryōtei.
14 Ryōtei is a type of luxurious traditional Japanese restaurant.
15 Chen Zu En, *Honkō ni atta nihon ryōriten*, 127 (2011).
16 Lu Xun and his common-law wife Xu Guangping lived in a succession of houses in the Jingyunli 景雲里 No. 17, 18, and 23 Hengbang, Lane 35, Hengbang Road (now East Hengbang Road 東横浜路). Between 1931 and 1933, they occasionally

lived hiding in the Ramos Apartments in a flat rented by Uchiyama Kanzō. April 11, 1933, they moved to a house Continental Terrace 大陆新邨 (No. 9, Lane 132, Shanyin Road), where they lived for the rest of Lu Xun's life. Lu Xun's youngest brother Zhou Jianren, an editor at Commercial Press, lived at Number 10 Jingyunli, Kaiming Press editor Ye Shengtao, lived at No. 11 Jingyunli. For a time, Mao Dun, then a budding novelist, lived with Ye at No. 11 Jingyunli. In 1928 Chen Wangdao and Wang Fuquan opened their Dajing Bookstore at No. 4 Jingyunli featuring literary and art magazines, Marxist publications, and the works of Lu Xun, Mao Dun, and other revolutionary writers. For a short time Guo Morou lived fewer than 500 meters away on No. 89, Lane 201, Doulun Road. All were near North Sichuan Road, north of the International Settlement, under direct Chinese control. Lu Xun's house in the Continental Terrace Development is now a museum. At this writing, all still exist. Near the entry gate of Jingyunli there is a small museum housed in a renovated shikumen house.

17 Maruyama Noboru, *Shanhai monogatari: Kokusai toshi shanhai to nitchū bunkajin*, 189.
18 Chen Zu En, *Shanhai ni ita nihonjin: Kaneko Mitsuharu to shanhai.*
19 Kaneko Mitsuharu, *Dokurohai*, 137-138.
20 Clarté Movement founded in France in 1919 by Henri Barbusse, was the first international writers' association. It was born out of hatred for war from experiences of WWI to oppose fascism and colonialism in sympathy with communism.
21 The aim of the 1925 Peace Preservation Law amendment was to suppress any political opposition. It gave the government carte blanche to outlaw any form of dissent. Those in leadership positions and those who participated in organization activities were subject to forced labor or prison for up to ten years.

22 Satomura Kinzō and Komaki Ōmi, "Seiten hakujitsu no kuni e," *Bungei sensen* (1927).
23 Wu Qishan 鄔其山 in Jon Eugene von Kowallis. *The Lyrical Lu Xun: A Study of His Classical Style Verse*, (Honolulu: University of Hawaii Press, 1995), 135.
24 Although it is normal for non-Chinese to adopt or be given a Chinese name, for a Japanese it becomes a tricky matter. The characters for Uchiyama in Chinese 內山 (Neishan) would automatically identify him as Japanese. The choice of Wu Qishan was a conscious attempt to fit in, to meet Chinese on their own terms, and finally to dissociate himself from Japan. Paul D. Scott. "Japanese Literary Travelers," *Chinese Studies in History*, 30, 4 (1997): 69.
25 Ozawa Masamoto, *Uchiyama Kanzō den: Nitchū yūkō ni tsukushita idai na shomin* (Tokyo: Banchō Shobō, 1972), 138.
26 Ozawa Masamoto, *Uchiyama Kanzō den: Nitchū yūkō ni tsukushita idai na shomin*, 140.
27 Uchiyama Shoten, "Uchiyama Shoten to Uchiyama Kanzō, "*Uchiyama* 3. (Tokyo: Uchiyama Shoten, 1985), 54.

FIFTH TURN OF THE KALEIDOSCOPE

A HAVEN
(1927-1936)

BETWEEN 1927 and 1936, China and Japan actively suppressed local communist cells and leftist organizations. The period also marked a shift in the role played by Uchiyama Bookstore. While the bookstore continued to serve as a fountain of knowledge and a Sino-Japanese cultural salon, it also became a haven for many of its Chinese and Japanese left-wing activist patrons.

Seeing cooperation with the other as a strategic advantage in their separate aims to control China, in 1924, the KMT and the CPC had formed the First United Front. The objective was to join forces to oust the Beijing-based warlord government and unite China under a CPC-influenced KMT-led government. Accordingly, the United Front formed the National Revolutionary Army (NRA). The NRA's 100,000-strong Northern Expedition under General Chiang Kai-shek set off from the south in 1926

NAOKO KATO

toward Beijing.

On May 15, 1925, a strike by Chinese workers at a Japanese-owned cotton spinning mill in Huxi 滬西, in the Chinese-controlled industrial districts north of the International Settlement (now Putuo district), had demonstrated the rising power of the communists and the labor movement. The strike, directed primarily toward Britain and Japan, ignited an anti-imperialist uprising and sparked a three-month-long general strike that spread to other parts of China and involved more than a million workers, students, and peasants.

In 1927, while the Northern Expedition had yet to complete its mission, forces loyal to Chiang Kai-shek and the KMT carried out a violent purge of communists and labor union activists. The purge, known as the Shanghai Massacre, began in Shanghai on April 12, 1927. It was conducted inside and outside the government and military, including the NRA. In Shanghai alone, some four thousand leftists were killed. The purge spread to other cities under KMT control, and countless others were killed.[1]

Following the Manchurian Incident on September 18, 1931, Japan's Kwantung Army[2] occupied Chinese-controlled Manchuria. In response, pro-and anti-Japanese sentiments ran high in Shanghai. Tens of thousands of Chinese students marched in the streets in protest, and segments of Shanghai's sizeable Japanese community were eager to counter the anti-Japanese demonstrations. At the same time, at high levels in both the Japanese Imperial Army and the civil government, some thought the time had come to elevate Japan's status vis-à-vis Western powers that controlled Shanghai's foreign concessions. Consequently, after taking control of Manchuria, the Japanese Imperial Army began to extend Japan's influence south to Shanghai with the concurrence of the civil government in Tokyo.

Chinese-owned Sanyou Industries Textile Factory was a

known center of anti-Japanese activism in the International Settlement's Yangpu district. To divert attention from the Manchurian Incident, local Japanese officials[3] arranged an attack on a group of Japanese monks as they passed near the factory gate on their daily rounds to receive alms.[4] A mob of Chinese quickly joined in beating the monks, killing one and seriously injuring two others. The Manchurian Incident had already stretched to the limit the tensions between Shanghai's Japanese community and Chinese residents. Street fighting erupted as the two groups engaged in attacks and counterattacks.

The opening battles on January 28, 1932, of the five-week-long Battle of Shanghai took place in the Hongkou district of the International Settlement. At midnight three thousand Japanese Special Naval Landing Force troops surged out of their barracks on North Sichuan Road and attacked Shanghai North Railway Station. The invasion spread throughout the de facto Japanese-controlled area encompassing Uchiyama Bookstore and the homes of the Uchiyamas, Lu Xun, and other Chinese and Japanese anti-government activists. Subsequent bombing of commercial and residential areas and fighting between troops, ships, and aircraft of the Japanese Imperial Army and troops under the auspices of the ROC spread into much of Chinese-controlled Shanghai. Fighting continued until the March 3 retreat of Chinese troops defending Shanghai.

During the fighting, Lu Xun and his family took refuge at the Fuzhou Road branch of Uchiyama Bookstore. Lu Xun's wife Xu Guangping 許廣平 (1898-1968) described the experience:

> February 1932, we finally escaped to Uchiyama's branch store (near) Fuzhou Road. When we were (in hiding) at the bookstore on North Sichuan Road, we saw how everybody at the store was in a state of chaos.

> We were enclosed in the small room upstairs and spent each day weary of the loud voices and cries that our children would make. We heard gunshots that rang in our ears and the sounds of the soldiers' footsteps even more clearly because everyone kept silent. On our national soil, we suffered through oppression that even the invaders would find suffocating. Nobody said a word, but our hearts communicated. Our indescribable emotions flooded our hearts in violent waves, becoming unbearable.[5]

May Fourth writers like Lu Xun, who in many ways led the War of Resistance against Japan, were pursued by authorities of the Chinese government for their leftist activities. In Japan, during this same period, proletarian literature and left-wing activism also flourished and were met with government suppression and mass arrests. As a result, some of these writers and activists fled to Shanghai, where they found a haven at Uchiyama Bookstore. Lu Xun was at the center of the bookstore's network of Sino-Japanese left-wing writers and activists until his death.

Uchiyama confided to Xu Guangping, "Even among Japanese, there are those who do not sell their friends to the enemy." She interpreted this to mean that Uchiyama guaranteed Lu Xun's protection. By choosing to protect Lu Xun, Uchiyama risked his own life. In the 1930s, the local Chinese government authorities suspected Uchiyama of spying for Japan or harboring left-wing radicals. Several times he and Miki evacuated to Japan. When the Japanese Consulate in Shanghai suspected Uchiyama of spying for the CPC, Lu Xun came to his defense, explaining that Uchiyama was merely a businessman who sold books. How can Uchiyama's decision to protect Lu Xun be explained? Was it motivated by the relationship between customer and bookstore owner? Between writer and publisher? Or even by friendship or sympathy? Instead, Uchiyama saw Lu Xun as a prophet, reformer, and full of fighting spirit for China. Uchiyama had become a disciple of Lu Xun.

To hide Lu Xun, Uchiyama rented as many as seven houses in his own name and some under the names of other Japanese. On three occasions, Uchiyama arranged for the evacuation of Lu Xun to a safe hiding place. The first followed the March 2, 1930, League of Left-Wing Writers (LLWW) founding meeting. Shortly after that, Shanghai authorities issued a warrant for Lu Xun's arrest. As a result, Lu Xun fled from his home on March 19, leaving Xu Guangping and their son Zhou Haiying behind. He took temporary refuge until April 1 in a room on the second floor of the Uchiyama Bookstore. In May, while Lu Xun was still a "wanted" man. Uchiyama rented an apartment in the Ramos Apartments on North Sichuan Road near the bookstore. From May 1930 until April 1933, Lu Xun lived off and on in the Ramos at Uchiyama's expense.[6] Others of Uchiyama's dissident friends also took refuge in the apartment from time to time.

The second occasion was in January 1931. On January 19, Uchiyama learned that the police had arrested Lu Xun's good friend Rou Shi 柔石 (1902-1931) and other LLWW members.[7] Uchiyama's friend Yoda, from the Japanese Christian Church, owned Hanazono Ryokan[8] on Huangdu Road off North Sichuan Road. Fearing for Lu Xun's safety, Uchiyama asked Yoda to hide Lu Xun as a guest. Yoda agreed. From January 20 through February 27, Lu Xun and his family hid in one of the small rooms in the ryokan. Meanwhile, on February 7, at Shanghai's Longhua Prison, the local government executed twenty-four of those arrested. Five of the twenty-four, including Rou Shi, are known as the Five Martyrs of the League of Left-Wing Writers. On Lu Xun's return home from hiding, his brother Zhou Jianren recalled that the nameplate hanging on the door read "Kamata Seiichi."

The third occasion in 1932 followed the January 28 Incident described earlier in this chapter. Lu Xun and his family were temporarily staying with Lu Xun's brother Zhou Jianren and his family in an apartment building on North Sichuan Road across the street from the Japanese Special Naval Landing Forces headquarters. On the evening of January 28, bullets flew. One put a hole in the wall next to Lu Xun's desk. Around dawn on January 30, someone in their apartment building fired a shot at the headquarters building. Japanese soldiers went door to door to investigate and came to Zhou Jianren's door. When Uchiyama learned of the soldiers' visit, he arranged to evacuate Lu Xun and his family from the International Settlement's Japanese community into a safer part of the city. Well-known in the Japanese community, Uchiyama inscribed a message in Japanese on business cards that he gave to Lu Xun: "I guarantee that this person is one of my acquaintances."

On January 30, the two families took refuge on the second floor of the Uchiyama Bookstore on North Sichuan Road. They spent five days there, as Xu Guangping described earlier in this chapter. Then, on February 6, the two families, ten people in all, moved to the bookstore's "Fuzhou Road" branch near in the International Settlement.[9] Until March 19, the two families of ten people occupied a single room. After safely settling Lu Xun and his family, Uchiyama temporarily fled to Japan and left Lu Xun in the care of his trusted shop assistant Kamata Seiichi. Uchiyama also left his flagship bookshop on North Sichuan Road in Kamata's care.

Lu Xun had amassed an extensive collection of leftist journals and Marxist-Leninist books. Keeping such a collection at home would have been dangerous. So instead, he stored all but books currently in use or recently purchased in his "secret reading room" on the second floor of a house on Liyang Road.[10] By 1933 his collection had outgrown the secret reading room, and he needed a larger space. Once again, Uchiyama and Kamata came to the rescue. Uchiyama rented a room for Lu Xun's collection on the second floor of Kamata's home.

In 1934, only a year later, Kamata Seiichi died. Kamata worked for Uchiyama from 1930, coinciding with the years during which Lu Xun's survival was most at risk. He was the "Kamata Seiichi" whose nameplate hung on the door of Lu Xun's home on his return from hiding in 1931. Lu Xun composed Kamata's epitaph.

Between 1927 and 1937, after the anti-communist purge and breakup of the First United Front, the government of the Republic of China, now controlled by the KMT, mounted several campaigns to exterminate the CPC. As a result, the authorities considered many among Uchiyama's customers to be political dissidents. Such people were subject to censorship and lived under the constant threat of kidnapping and arrest. During this period, Uchiyama provided a haven for Guo Moruo and Lu Xun.

Guo was among the left-wing writers who had joined the Northern Expedition. During the Shanghai Massacre and subsequent purge of communists and labor union activists, Guo left the Northern Expedition and sought refuge at the Uchiyama Bookstore. While hiding at the bookstore, Guo published poems and wrote about the transition from literary revolution to revolutionary literature. While disclosing neither Uchiyama's name nor the name of the bookstore, Guo recounts an event that took place in July 1927 as he waited for his comrade Xin at "a bookstore located on North Sichuan Road." The passage hints at the dangerous situation in which Guo found himself and the trust between him and the Uchiyamas.

When I entered the bookstore, the owner (Uchiyama) led me to the back and updated me on Shanghai's situation and the Japanese attitudes towards us. I also told him everything without withholding anything. The owner would always run upstairs to inform me of any Chinese who came to buy books downstairs. His wife would mediate for us. She would whisper in my ears since she knew my hearing was not very good: "There is a Chinese person who came to buy a book. He probably knows your face, so don't come downstairs."[11]

Guo came out of hiding to join the CPC's forces of the August 1, 1927, Nanchang Uprising. The uprising, which followed the Chinese government's purge of communists earlier in the year, ended in the CPC's defeat. It was the first significant KMT-CPC engagement of the Chinese Civil War. Communist forces abandoned control of Nanchang and withdrew into the Jinggang Mountains of western Jiangxi; thus, the Long March began. Guo fled to Shanghai and once again took refuge at Uchiyama Bookstore.

The Chinese government's Emergency Law of March 7, 1928, stipulated that the authorities would "severely punish anyone who spread doctrines incompatible with the KMT." The law aimed to prevent people like Guo Moruo from disseminating communist or "reactionary" propaganda. However, the law did not dampen Guo's activism. Once again, in December 1928, Uchiyama came to Guo's rescue and assisted in his escape to Japan. Hiding from authorities in a house on Duolun Road, Guo intended to join the remaining staff of the Shanghai Soviet Embassy and board the last ship departing for Moscow. Suddenly, the night before the ship's departure, he fell ill with typhus and was forced to remain in Shanghai for two weeks of treatment at Dr. Ishii's hospital on

North Sichuan Road. Consequently, Guo had no choice but to change his destination to Japan. One step ahead of the police the night before Guo's departure, Uchiyama moved him from the Ishii Hospital to Yashiro Ryokan. Uchiyama saw Guo off from Nippon Yūsen's Wayside Wharf the following morning.

Uchiyama arranged with Tanaka Keitarō, owner of Bunkyūdō bookstore in Tokyo, for Guo to make a living in Japan. For the next ten years under Tanaka, Guo not only published numerous works through Bunkyūdō but also became a regular at Bunkyūdō's cultural salon. In return for Tanaka's favor, in China, Uchiyama sold about half of the books published by Bunkyūdō, including many Japanese language textbooks, which he sold to Shanghai's Japanese schools. As for Guo, during his exile in Japan, whenever he sent manuscripts to China, he always addressed them to Uchiyama Bookstore.

Along with providing a haven for dissidents like Guo Moruo and Lu Xun, Uchiyama and his bookstore ensured that some of China's rare Buddhist scriptures escaped destruction. For example, Xia Mianzun of Kaiming Press and Uchiyama's regular customer approached Uchiyama in 1927:

> I have somebody that I want to introduce you to, so could you come when I phone you." A few days later, he rang. The meeting place was on Beijing Road at Gongdelin 功德林.[12] By the time I got there, everybody was waiting. I apologized for being late and sat down. Over ten people were sitting on both sides of a rectangular table. Most of them were my customers, so it was a very relaxing meeting. I sat next to a monk across from Xia. Xia immediately introduced me to the monk, Li Shutong (Buddhist name Hong Yi 弘一).[13]

Li Shutong 李叔同 (1880-1942) had discovered, organized, compiled, and published a one hundred-twenty-volume series of Buddhist scriptures. Xia asked Uchiyama to distribute two hundred-thirty sets of these newly published volumes to Japanese temples. Later, Li discovered a group of twenty-five volumes of wooden printing blocks—forty-eight books comprised each volume. Surmising that these were examples of China's oldest wooden printing blocks, Li felt these were unsafe in China and desperately wanted the original collection sent to Japan for safekeeping. However, before sending originals to Japan for safekeeping, Li reproduced twenty-five copies. Uchiyama arranged the shipment of fifteen copies of each volume to Japan's universities, temples, and libraries.

Between 1927 and 1936, Japanese writers working in both Japan and Shanghai translated several of Lu Xun's works into Japanese. Just as Lu Xun eagerly passed his ideas on to young Chinese writers, some trustworthy young Japanese writers became his disciples. Masuda Wataru and Kaji Wataru were two Japanese writers to whom Lu Xun gave private sessions on Chinese literature. Between 1927 and 1936, Lu Xun was in hiding for long periods and had very few visitors, so he had ample time to devote to facilitating the translation of his work into Japanese.

Masuda Wataru was a scholar of Chinese literature and studied translation under Japanese novelist and poet Satō Haruo. During his 1927 trip to Shanghai, Satō visited Uchiyama Bookstore and met Uchiyama. When Masuda set off for Shanghai in 1931, he carried a letter of introduction from Satō addressed to Uchiyama. Aware of Lu Xun's habit of stopping by the bookstore on his afternoon walks, Masuda went there, and Uchiyama introduced him to Lu Xun.

At the suggestion of Uchiyama, Masuda agreed to translate Lu Xun's *The History of Chinese Fiction*. From March through

December of 1931, Masuda went to Lu Xun's house every afternoon for a three-hour-long session on Chinese literature. Lu Xun and Masuda devoted the first three months of their sessions entirely to this one book. After returning to Japan, Masuda corresponded with Lu Xun by letters and continued to question Lu Xun on how best to interpret specific passages. In 1935, Masuda published Lu Xun's selected works in Japanese, and in years to come, he translated many pieces of Lu Xun's writings.

Kaji Wataru was the only other Japanese to study Chinese literature with Lu Xun. Kaji was among the Japanese Proletarian Federation of Artists founders in 1928. He joined the JCP in 1932 and, in 1934, was arrested and charged with propagating communism. However, he was released in 1935 after renouncing his Marxist ideology and publicly subscribing to the Japanese state (*tenkō*). After that, he was under constant police surveillance and required to report to the police and the courthouse whenever he moved, even within Tokyo.

The early 1930s were not only a time of mass arrests for Japanese communists, but their lives were also at stake. For example, two years before Rou Shi's execution in Shanghai, in February 1933, proletarian writer Kobayashi Takiji (1903-1933), who had invited Kaji to join the Communist Party, was tortured to death by Japanese military police. In his memoir, Kaji wrote of his wish to find a place to die amid the struggle between the Japanese invasion and Chinese liberation. In January 1936, disguised as a member of actor Tōyama Mitsuru's[14] China tour, Kaji escaped from Japan to China. He arrived in Shanghai friendless and exhausted from his fight to find a way out of his "failures." Carrying a letter of introduction, he went straight to Uchiyama Bookstore, where he met Uchiyama. He explained his situation and asked for Uchiyama's help finding inconspicuous work.

A few days later, through Uchiyama, Kaji met Lu Xun. In

turn, Lu Xun introduced Kaji to Hu Feng 胡風 (1902-1985), who had studied in Japan and was a member of the LLWW. Then, at Uchiyama Bookstore, Kaji met left-wing literary pioneer and Creation Society member Zheng Boqi. Finally, through Zheng, Kaji met playwright/screenwriter Xia Yan, a fellow Communist Party member. During Kaji's stay in Shanghai, Xia became one of his best friends. These encounters all occurred within a week of Kaji's meeting with Uchiyama. They suggested how easily, with the help of Uchiyama, information traveled through Shanghai's network of like-minded activists.

After hearing Lu Xun utter the names of his comrades in Japan and learning of Lu Xun's intimate knowledge of the Japanese labor and liberation movements, Kaji was overcome with joy. Nevertheless, Kaji told Lu Xun that he intended never to return to Japan. Lu Xun replied that it would be necessary for Kaji to make a living and maintain legal status, yet never discussed how the matter would be handled. Instead, Lu Xun consulted Uchiyama, who stepped forward to act as Kaji's guarantor to the Japanese authorities. As a result, Kaji was to stay out of Shanghai political matters and, instead, study Chinese literature under Lu Xun. Later, Kaji learned that he was safe from Shanghai's Japanese civil and military police because of Uchiyama's involvement.

Lu Xun put Kaji to work on a Japanese translation of new Chinese literary works for Kaizōsha Publishing House. Uchiyama wrote to his friend Yamamoto Sanehiko, president of Kaizōsha, suggesting that he include a translation of a new Chinese literary work in each issue of Kaizōsha's monthly general-interest magazine *Kaizō*. Yamamoto agreed, and each of the magazine's following five editions contained translations by Kaji.

While Kaji was working with Lu Xun on the translation of the third piece, Lu Xun's health rapidly deteriorated. When the project became too physically demanding for Lu Xun, Hu Feng replaced him and came from his home in the French Concession twice each week to work with Kaji. Uchiyama's journalist friend Hidaka Kiyomasa, an alumnus of EACCA, was fluent in Chinese, and Uchiyama arranged for Hidaka to assist Kaji with translation. Together Hidaka and Kaji translated parts of *Collected Works of Lu Xun* published after Lu Xun's death.

Many people chose to leave Shanghai after the Shanghai War of 1932 and the resulting increase in Japan's control over eastern China. Kaji left Shanghai first for Hong Kong, then following the Chinese government and his Shanghai friends, he went to Wuhan and later to Chongqing. In December 1938, in Wuhan, Kaji and Guo Moruo established the Japanese People's Anti-War Alliance to "educate" Japanese POWs to fight for the communist cause in Japan. When the KMT-led Chinese government invited Kaji to work for the government's anti-Japan propaganda campaigns, it fit right into his plans. Carrying orders from the KMT, he went to Guilin to visit POW camps, interviewed Japanese prisoners, and recruited those he deemed suitable into the Anti-War League.

China specialist, left-wing Japanese journalists Ozaki Hotsumi 尾崎秀実 (1901-1944) and Yamagami Masayoshi 山上正義 (1896-1938) were Uchiyama Bookstore regulars who also translated Lu Xun's works into Japanese. Ozaki Hotsumi arrived in Shanghai in November 1928 as a journalist for *Asahi News*. Through his relationship with Uchiyama and the bookstore, he met and established relationships with members of the Creation Society. He was particularly close to Society member Tao Jingsun, who, in the early 1930s, introduced him to Lu Xun. Yamagami Masayoshi was Chief of the China Section of United Press. In 1921, before coming to China, he had been arrested and imprisoned for eight months in Tokyo for propagating communism. Then, in 1925, he came to China as a reporter for United Press.

The following year, Yamagami's friend Kakinohara Toyoko

moved from Tokyo to Shanghai. She rented a flat in Magnolia Terrace,[15] where she lived and operated a hair salon. Then in 1927, the Creation Society moved its office from the International Settlement to Magnolia Terrace. The area was under Chinese jurisdiction and off-limits to International Settlement police. In relative safety from the police of either the local Chinese government or the International Settlement, Creation Society members such as Zheng Boqi and Tao Jingsun "hung out" at the Society's office.

In 1927 United Press sent Yamagami to Guangzhou to report on happenings in Guangdong province. While in Guangzhou, he met Lu Xun and members of the Creation Society. While there, he wrote about Lu Xun, began translating Lu Xun's *The True Story of Ah Q*, and covered the failed Guangzhou Uprising of November 1927. When Yamagami returned from Guangzhou to Shanghai in 1929, he and Kakinohara lived together at her place in Magnolia Terrace and later married. Yamagami often joined his Creation Society friends who gathered at the Society's Magnolia Terrace office. It was here that he and Ozaki met. Together, Yamagami and Ozaki completed the translation of *The True Story of Ah Q*. They dedicated it to the "Martyrs of the Longhua Incident of 1931."

Through Tao Jingsun and other patrons of Uchiyama Bookstore, Ozaki and Yamagami had met not only Creation Society members but also other left-wing Chinese activists. The two assisted these activists in finding safe gathering places for their activities. For example, the Shanghai Art and Drama Society[16] was exploring alternatives to proletariat literature that would better communicate their message of revolution to ordinary Chinese people. The Society planned to stage an adaptation of Erich Maria Remarque's 1929 anti-war novel *All Quiet on the Western Front* and needed a revolving stage. The only venue with a suitable stage was a Japanese-owned *kabuki* theater. Yamagami arranged for Xia and his group to stage the performance in the *kabuki* theater. In May 1930, Xia sought Ozaki's help finding a place where forty to fifty LLWW members could gather without being noticed. That month Ozaki was hosting the monthly meeting of Shanghai's Japanese journalists. Having already arranged a meeting space for the day of his event, Ozaki allowed Xia to hold the League meeting there at a different time of the day.

Ozaki Hotsumi was born in Japan but grew up in Taiwan. His father, Hotsuma worked as a journalist for the Japanese-controlled *Taiwan Daily News* and produced the Chinese version of the newspaper as well. Growing up in a literati household, Ozaki was steeped in classical Japanese and Chinese literature. He was also versed in history and wrote classical Chinese poetry. In 1922, Ozaki enrolled in Tokyo Imperial University to study law. However, in the aftermath of the Great Kantō Earthquake of 1923, he observed extreme right-wing groups engaged in vigilante killings of ethnic Koreans and leftists whom they blamed for looting. Appalled by this experience, he turned to Marxism and became involved in the activities of the JCP.

Ozaki joined the Asahi News in 1926 as a journalist, and in 1928 the newspaper sent him to Shanghai. By this time, Ozaki believed that a Pan-Asian Society allying with the Soviet Union, a post-Capitalist Japan, and China under the leadership of CPC would rid East Asia of Western colonialism. Soon after arriving in Shanghai, Ozaki connected with left-wing journalist Agnes Smedley (1892-1950). Then in 1930, she introduced him to German journalist Richard Sorge (1894-1944). Sorge was an undercover military intelligence officer of the Soviet Union working under the Comintern. The Comintern charged Sorge and his spy ring with gathering information on German and

Japanese plans to attack the Soviet Union. Ozaki agreed to assist Sorge by collecting data on internal Chinese politics and Japan's Manchurian plans. Ozaki believed that by carrying out this activity, he could contribute to the anti-imperialist objectives of the Chinese revolution.

In Shanghai, Ozaki also established connections with left-wing EACCA students. Between 1920 and 1934, Chinese students studied at EACCA alongside students from Japan. All EACCA students lived in dormitories on campus. Beginning in 1928, Chinese and Japanese students were housed together rather than separately. Thus, living side-by-side Chinese and Japanese students formed a tightly knit community.

Consequently, EACCA became a hotbed of radicalism. The close relationships among students led many Japanese to join their Chinese classmates in supplementing EACCA lectures on practical knowledge, such as Chinese transportation and geography, with study to address China's real problems. Students formed reading groups to study socialism and Marxism and frequented Uchiyama Bookstore to buy books on the topics. They were attracted to the bookstore by the availability of books, many forbidden in Japan, lively discussions, and Uchiyama's policy of loaning books and selling on credit. As a result, there were left-wing books in every EACCA dormitory room.

Students also formed the China Problem Research Group, which Ozaki and Marxist economist Wang Xuewen 王學文 (1895-1985) tutored. The CPC had tapped Wang to recruit anti-imperialist and anti-war Japanese in Shanghai. In November 1930, the Research Group and another group consisting mainly of journalists joined and formed the Japan-China Struggle League. The League's primary objective was to disseminate anti-war slogans directed at the Japanese Special Naval Landing Force crew members.

KALEIDOSCOPE

One night, League members wrote large character slogans along walls that crew members would pass when training the following day. They wrote with coal tar, making the slogans almost impossible to erase:

> Down with Japanese Imperialism!
> Join hands with China's Soviets!
> Reverse your Guns!
> Knock Down the Nation of Capitalist Landowners!
> Long Live the Communist Party of China!
> Long Live Soldiers, Laborers, Farmers!
> Japan-China Struggle League[17]

The next day it was a big story in newspapers all over Shanghai. They ran articles with pictures of the slogans prominently highlighting the Japan-China Struggle League. Then, in December, the Japanese Embassy police raided dormitory rooms, confiscated left-wing books, and arrested eight EACCA student members of the League.

With the onset in January 1932 of the month-long Battle of Shanghai between the Chinese and Imperial Japan troops, many Japanese feared for their safety and evacuated to Japan. Ozaki left Shanghai temporarily in February 1932 to work at Asahi News in Osaka. Yamagami left Shanghai in November 1932 for a position at United Press in Beijing. However, Uchiyama had no intention of leaving, as reflected in the war reportage of journalist Muramatsu Shōfū titled "Amidst Shanghai's Fire in War:"

> A tatami mat is placed around the front (of Uchiyama Bookstore) to prevent bullets from flying inside. Looking further in, I see a glass door. As I entered, the Uchiyamas and another lady sat by the *hibachi* at

the back of the store. The close-cropped-headed store owner (Uchiyama), wearing a woolen sweater, stood up with astonishment and greeted me, "My gosh, what a visitor I have here!"[18]

After the Battle of Shanghai, Ozaki returned to Shanghai. Then in 1934, he returned for good to Japan, where, with Sorge, he continued intelligence-gathering activities. In 1937, Shōwa Research Association (Shōwa Kenkyūkai) recruited Ozaki to serve in a think tank established by Prime Minister Konoe Fumimaro. From 1938, he was a member of Konoe's inner circle of advisors and participated in its decision-making. Through Sorge, he continued to provide reports to the Soviet Union.

From 1939, Ozaki served as a high-level consultant to the Japanese-controlled South Manchurian Railway. Ozaki's father and the head of the railway's research group had worked together in Taiwan. Through this connection, Ozaki arranged for the appointment of left-wing members to the group. From these appointees, he collected and passed on to Sorge information on Japan's plans in Manchuria.

Ozaki Hotsumi never became a Communist Party member. Nonetheless, he continued to work for Sorge until the arrest of both in October 1941 on suspicion of engaging in espionage. In November 1944, the Japanese government executed him and Sorge. Ozaki's social networks with left-wing Chinese writers and activists through Uchiyama Bookstore enabled him to realize his larger objectives. Still, there is no evidence that Uchiyama was ever a communist or interested in Ozaki's political activities. On the contrary, historian Joshua Fogel describes Uchiyama as "apolitical," a nearly impossible position to maintain under the extremely political circumstances of the time.[19]

From the late 1920s through the late 1930s, both the Nationalist government of China and the Empire of Japan conducted violent persecutions of left-wing writers and activists. Therefore, it was a risky undertaking for Lu Xun to give private lessons to Japanese left-wing writers and translators. However, his motivation could not have been to pass the time during his hiding. Just as Lu Xun was eager to share his ideas with young Chinese writers, he also viewed a few trustworthy young Japanese writers as his disciples. Likewise, Japanese left-wing activists such as Ozaki Hotsumi and Kaji Wataru risked persecution by fighting alongside their Chinese counterparts against Japanese imperialism.

From the end of the 1920s to the early 1930s, radicalism emerged in the visual arts. It took its place alongside radical activism promulgated through works of literature, journalism, vernacular theater, and public speaking. For example, in 1929, the Nationalist-controlled government of China sponsored the *National Fine Arts Exhibition*. In response, societies such as the Art Movement Society and Eighteen Art Society[20] formed to counter the conservatism that the *National Fine Arts Exhibition* espoused.

In the context of visual art-related radical activism, the New Woodcut Movement emerged in China, with Lu Xun as its pre-eminent promoter. The woodcut print had been a popular Chinese art form for more than a millennium. Then, in the early 20th century, Chinese progressives began to promote the woodcut print for its Chinese roots and its use in the West to advocate for social change. Lu Xun was among the first to examine foreign woodcut prints and recognize the medium's potential to promote social change in China. He saw in woodcut prints the evocative power to bridge the literacy gap and awaken the Chinese masses in a way that literature could not.

Although the woodblock print was an indigenous craft and artform, modern woodcut printmaking in China returned to China through its offshoots that had taken root in Japan.

NAOKO KATO

In August 1931, Lu Xun and Uchiyama organized a hands-on woodcut printmaking workshop in a classroom at Uchiyama's Japanese Language School. Uchiyama's brother Kakichi came from Tokyo to teach the craft, and Lu Xun served as Kakichi's translator.

Under Lu Xun's influence, the woodcut print became a widespread public art form across Chinese society. The CPC adopted woodcut images as propaganda tools in mobilizing peasants to fight against the KMT as the two opposing sides struggled to control China. By the early 1930s, Chinese radical woodcut artists and radical activists of all other types faced intense suppression and persecution by authorities of the Chinese government. Exhibits were banned, artists jailed and their work confiscated, and many visual art-related societies were forced to disband.

While Lu Xun had a life-long interest in the visual arts, his profound engagement with the visual arts began in 1927, after he arrived in Shanghai. He realized that the Chinese lacked a foundation for creating new art and that systematic study of modern art could provide the foundation. He encouraged Uchiyama to order art history books in Japanese and then translated and published them. Lu Xun continued purchasing and studying foreign art books and built an extensive personal collection. Besides books on art, he collected prints created by artists worldwide. Over time, his collection grew to four hundred such pieces.

In 1928, Lu Xun began editing *The Current*, a journal committed to publishing translations of articles from foreign journals on art and literary criticism. Selecting visual material for each issue was one of his responsibilities. Since the mid-1920s, Chinese journals had already begun publishing reproductions of woodcuts as modern art forms. So, from 1929, Lu Xun began selecting woodcut prints from his collection to run in *The Current* and other magazines.

Lu Xun had built his collection of art books and prints by asking Chinese students studying in Europe to ship items to him at Uchiyama Bookstore. On delivery of shipments, Lu Xun showed the contents to Uchiyama and Miki. On one occasion, Uchiyama expressed interest in exhibiting pieces from Lu Xun's collection, "I would like to exhibit these woodcut prints you've been collecting. Would you mind lending them to me so that I can organize an exhibit?" Lu Xun agreed and selected and framed around seventy works by German and Russian artists and prepared placards for each piece with the name and country of the artist in both the original language and Chinese.

The first exhibit of works from Lu Xun's collection took place in October 1930 on the second floor of the Japanese language school operated by Uchiyama on Liyang Road. Some four hundred people, mainly Japanese, attended the two-day exhibit. Unfortunately, this exhibit attracted few Chinese, so Uchiyama and Lu Xun deemed it only a semi-success. In Autumn 1932, there was a second exhibit of the works at the Japanese YMCA. Again, attendance was low, and Lu Xun and Uchiyama also considered it a failure. The third exhibit of the pieces in October 1933 took place in Qianaili, the lane in which the Uchiyamas lived, and attracted Chinese and Japanese. Even Chinese elementary school children visited. Both men dubbed the exhibit a success.

Uchiyama and Lu Xun also helped exhibit other woodcut print collections during this period. In June 1931, Lu Xun learned through his friend poet Feng Xuefeng 馮雪峰 (1903-1976) that the Eighteen Arts Society was eager to promote woodcut prints but was struggling to do so. So, Uchiyama arranged with Japanese Daily News to rent the second floor of its Hongkou headquarters for the exhibition.

Lu Xun learned that a piece from his collection titled "Cement" by Carl Meffert (1903–1988), a Swiss/German politically and socially conscious graphic designer and artist, had appeared in *The Current*. The piece had inspired artists Jiang Feng 江豐 (1910-1982) and Chen Tiegeng 陳鐵耕 (1908-1969). Since there were no woodcut print teachers in China, the two taught themselves by studying the work of Meffert. Other young artists introduced to woodcut prints through exhibits and journal publications were also attempting to teach themselves by studying examples. Lu Xun harbored a long-held dream of teaching Chinese artists the craft. The time was now ripe for a hands-on workshop.

In August 1931, the opportunity for Lu Xun to turn his dream into reality presented itself. From Tokyo, Uchiyama's younger brother Kakichi and his wife Matsumo were visiting the Uchiyamas. In his memoir, Kakichi captures the occasion's atmosphere and highlights the significance of the encounter in developing China's New Woodcut Art Movement. Kakichi recalled, "after breakfast on August 6, 1931, Matsumo, Miki, and I were chatting. Kanzō joined us and handed me three postcards, which the postman had just delivered: "These are from your students. I think they are woodcut prints."

Keenly interested, Miki asked how one makes these postcards. Kakichi demonstrated how to carve an image onto a woodblock using some simple tools he had brought from Tokyo. As Matsumo practiced, Uchiyama told of the woodcut exhibit he and Lu Xun had organized the previous autumn. At that moment, Lu Xun arrived at the bookstore for his daily visit. He joined the group in examining the postcards and observing Kakichi's impromptu woodblock carving and printmaking lesson. Then, impulsively, Lu Xun asked Kakichi for a favor; "Could you teach art students in Shanghai how to make woodcut prints?"

At first, Kakichi hesitated, explaining that he was not a

professional artist but a mere elementary schoolteacher. Then, after much persuasion from Lu Xun, Uchiyama, and Miki, he agreed. Lu Xun responded, "I will gather some students in the next few days," and hurriedly left the bookstore.[21]

Promptly, Lu Xun and Uchiyama organized the workshop. It took place from August 17 to 22 in classrooms of Uchiyama's Japanese language school on Changchun Road (長春路316號). Lu Xun recruited six members from the Eighteen Arts Society, two from Shanghai Arts College, two from Shanghai Art Academy, and three from the White Goose Western Painting Club. In all, thirteen students participated in the six-day workshop. Each morning Kakichi lectured for two hours in Japanese with Lu Xun interpreting. Afternoons Kakichi supervised hands-on activities. The first four days focused on black and white prints, with color added during the final two days. A student recalled:

> When Lu Xun entered the room along with the Japanese teacher, we cheered and clapped. Lu Xun was very moved and introduced the teacher as the Uchiyama Bookstore owner's brother, on vacation from Japan. He is a woodcut teacher and will teach you woodcut techniques—a rare opportunity for all of you. Therefore, I ask that you take these lectures seriously. Whenever we had extra time left, Lu Xun would critique works by overseas artists. We were particularly impressed by those of Käthe Kollwitz[22] and Japanese *ukiyoe*, which Kakichi supplemented with explanations of historical development in Japan. Kakichi repeatedly warned us to begin with simple projects and not hastily attempt to create complex scenes.[23]

Soon after the workshop, printmaking clubs sprang up, and Lu Xun began mentoring young printmakers. For example, workshop attendees Jiang Feng of the White Goose Western Painting Club, Chen Tiegeng of the Shanghai Arts College, and Chen Zhuokun 陳卓堃 (1908-2002) of the Eighteen Arts Society formed the Modern Woodcut Research Society. After that, however, printmaking clubs were born and rapidly died due to frequent arrests of printmaking artists and the political suppression of their organizations and exhibits.

Even so, both Lu Xun and Uchiyama continued to support the emerging New Woodcut Movement by organizing woodcut exhibitions and promoting the work of young Chinese woodcut artists. For example, Uchiyama Bookstore carried copies of woodcut print collections by Lu Xun's student Liu Xian 劉峴 (1915-1990) and by Liu's friend Huang Xinbo 黃新波 (1916-1980), who studied at the Imperial Arts College in Tokyo. Additionally, the bookstore carried *Modern Woodcut*, a periodical published by the Modern Woodcut Research Society, founded in 1934 by Li Hua 李樺 (1907-1994) at the Guangzhou Art School. The bookstore also served as a safe repository for woodcuts delivered there to Lu Xun from Shanghai, other parts of China, and abroad. In 1934, Lu Xun organized an exhibit in Paris titled "Painters and Printmakers from Revolutionary China." It was the first exhibition of modern Chinese woodcut prints outside of China.

The second annual *National Traveling Woodcut Exhibition* organized by the Modern Creative Print Society opened in Guangzhou on July 5, 1936. After Guangzhou, the Exhibition traveled to Shanghai, opened on October 2 at the Shanghai YMCA, and ran through October 8. A few days before his death on October 8, Lu Xun visited the exhibition, one of the eighty thousand people who attended during the Exhibition's run. One of the most evocative images on display was a black-and-white woodcut by Li Hua. The piece depicted a naked man, blindfolded, tightly bound to a stake, screaming while reaching for a dagger on the ground. The print titled " Roar, China!" is now widely regarded as a masterpiece in modern Chinese art, demonstrating the expressive capacity of a woodcut print and effectively articulating the national psyche.

Deteriorating health and the constant threat of arrest forced Lu Xun to live in seclusion and often in hiding. Many of his friends, including Uchiyama, Masuda Wataru, Agnes Smedley, and his physician Doctor Sudō, tried to persuade him to move from Shanghai to a safer place, even Japan. Undeterred, Lu Xun protested that because China needed him, he could not leave. While others were dying around him, somebody must stay in China and fight for the Chinese people. "I see China's future as the Arabian Desert—that is why I must continue to fight." With the desert fast approaching, leaving his country for personal safety was not an option.[24]

On October 18, 1936, Xu Guangping delivered a message to Uchiyama from her husband. Lu Xun wrote that since midnight, asthma had made his breathing difficult. He apologized for being unable to make their 10:00 AM appointment. He asked Uchiyama to phone Doctor Sudō and tell him to come. This message was the last Lu Xun wrote. The next day, October 19, 1936, Lu Xun died.

Lu Xun's obituary ran in both Japanese and Chinese newspapers and listed eight funeral committee members: Sun Yat-sen's widow Song Qingling (1893-1981); educator Cai Yuanpei (1868-1940); American journalist Agnes Smedley; writers Hu Yuzhi 胡愈之 (1896-1986) and Mao Dun; and Uchiyama Kanzō. Six thousand people attended the October 22 funeral, during which Uchiyama delivered the eulogy.

In his formal tribute, Uchiyama recounted the words of Lu

Xun indelibly inscribed in his mind and painted a powerful image of the critical work remaining for Lu Xun's survivors:

> A road is not there from the beginning, but only appears after a person walks along it. Recalling Lu Xun's words, I vividly see him quietly walking alone in the wilderness, leaving his footprints. May we not let weeds cover Lu Xun's footprints. Instead, let us strive with all our might to create from Lu Xun's footprints a wide road.[25]

Then, led by Lu Xun's casket draped in a white flag inscribed with the words "Soul of the People" (民族魂), the long funeral procession wound its way along streets lined with mourners to Universal Public Cemetery (萬國公墓).

Lu Xun was a mighty presence in this world. In a word, he was a prophet — a voice crying in the wilderness.

KALEIDOSCOPE

Endnotes:
1 The massacre marked the end of the First United Front and the uneasy cooperation of the KMT and the CPC in resisting Japanese aggression. Following the incident, conservative KMT elements purged communists in all areas under KMT control and evidently highlighted the split of the KMT into left- and right-wing factions.
2 The Kwantung Army was the largest unit of the Imperial Japanese Army. Between 1919 and 1945, it supported Japanese interests in China, Manchuria, and Mongolia.
3 Postwar, Major Tanaka Ryūichi, Japanese Special Services and Military Attaché to the Japanese Consulate in Shanghai, claimed that he organized the Shanghai Incident under the orders of Kwantung Army General Itagaki Seishirō, who was also behind the planning of the Manchurian Incident.
4 In Buddhism, alms or almsgiving is the respect given by a lay Buddhist to a Buddhist monk or nun.
5 Yoshida Hiroji, *Rojin no tomo Uchiyama Kanzō no shōzō*, 137.
6 Ramos Apartments, now Beichuan Apartments, 2093 North Sichuan Road 四川北路2093號.
7 During the 1930s, it was common for the local Chinese government Public Security Bureau and the Municipal Police of the International Settlement and the French Concession to collaborate. The KMT-led local government prioritized subjugating their internal CPC enemies over external Japanese enemies. The French were concerned about Indochinese communist revolutionaries, and the Municipal Council of the International Settlement was concerned about left-leaning Indian nationalists. Comintern agents from the Soviet Union were actively promulgating communism among these anti-imperialist revolutionary nationalists. This situation led concession police forces to maintain constant communication

with the local government and its Public Security Bureau in their mutual efforts to suppress communist activities in Shanghai.

8 A ryokan is a traditional Japanese inn with tatami-matted rooms, sliding door and window coverings, and communal baths.

9 The "Fuzhou Road" branch operated between 1930 and 1933 in the International Settlement at 215 Sichuan Middle Road between Fuzhou Road and Hongkou Road near The Bund. Its customers were primarily businesspeople who worked in the area. It was only open during lunch hours.

10 1359 Liyang Road 溧陽路1359號

11 Kaku Matsujaku, *Hokubatsu no tojō de, hoka, Kaku Matsujaku jiden*, (Tokyo: Heibonsha, 1987), 197.

12 Gongdelin (Godley) is a Buddhist vegetarian restaurant established in Shanghai in 1922, frequented by Japanese patrons and serving as a place to network. Writers Matsumoto Shōfū and Tanizaki Junichirō, as well as publisher Yamamoto Sanehiko were among Godelin's customers.

13 Uchiyama Kanzō, *Shanhai ringo*, 59.

14 The actor Tōyama Mitsuru is not to be mistaken with the Pan-Asianist rōnin Tōyama Mitsuru.

15 Magnolia Terrace was a majority Japanese-occupied lane-house community at 1811 North Sichuan Road. It was comprised of residences and small business and located a few blocks south of Uchiyama Bookstore at 2048 North Sichuan Road.

16 The Shanghai Art and Drama Society was founded in October 1929 by Xia Yan, Tao Jingsun, and others.

17 Ozaki, *Shanhai 1930-nen*, 131.

18 Yoshida Hiroji, *Rojin no tomo Uchiyama Kanzō no shōzō*, 129.

19 Joshua Fogel, "Integrating into Chinese Society: A Comparison

of Japanese Communities of Shanghai and Harbin," in *Japanese Competing Modernities: Issues in Culture and Democracy 1900-1930*, ed. Sharon A. Minichiello (Honolulu: University of Hawaii Press, 1998), 57.

20 The Art Movement Society was founded in 1928 by Lin Fengmian 林風眠 (1900-1991), pioneer of modern art in China and first director of the National Academy of Art, Hangzhou. The Eighteen Art Society was founded by students of the China Academy of Art in Hangzhou (aka China National Academy of Fine Arts).

21 Uchiyama Kakichi and Nara Kazuo, *Rojin to mokkō* (Tokyo: Kenbun Shuppan, 1981), 17.

22 Käthe Kollwitz (1867-1945) was a German woodcut print artists whose work Lu Xun greatly admired. She was a pacifist who portrayed laborers, those in poverty, and the human conditions of war. A collection of her works, which Lu Xun published in 1936, was his last graphic art-related publication.

23 Uchiyama Kakichi and Nara Kazuo, *Rojin to mokkō*, 194-195.

24 Uchiyama Kanzō, *Rojin no omoide*, 25.

25 Uchiyama Kanzō, *Rojin no omoide*, 23.

Sixth Turn of the Kaleidoscope

Searching for Peace Amidst War (1925-1945)

THE SECOND BATTLE of Shanghai, from mid-August to late November 1937, marked the beginning of the Second Sino-Japanese War[1] and yet another shift in the role of Uchiyama Bookstore. The Uchiyamas, like many Japanese residents of the Hongkou district, feared for their lives and evacuated to Japan during the three-month-long battle. Except for a few devoted "regulars," the bookstore's Chinese customers all but vanished. Kaji Wataru, was one such "regular." He dropped by the bookstore during the fighting to gather information and recalled:

> Customers purchasing books had disappeared; only Japanese neighbors in fear for their safety, and unidentifiable suspicious-looking customers came one after the other, sat down to talk, and then left.[2]

KALEIDOSCOPE

On October 19, 1937, the first anniversary of Lu Xun's death, a few close friends visited his grave. At the tomb, they found a fresh bouquet of chrysanthemums. Feng Xuefeng wondered, "Is Uchiyama still in Shanghai?" Even these close friends were unaware that Uchiyama had left for Japan. Kaji's wife replied, "When you mentioned chrysanthemums, I thought it would be him."[3]

With Imperial Japan's growing incursion into China, Shanghai's Japanese civilian population increased dramatically. In 1926 Japanese nationals numbered twenty thousand out of Shanghai's total population of 2.7 million. By 1939 the city's Japanese population had more than doubled to fifty-one thousand, and by 1943 it doubled again to more than one hundred thousand, outnumbering Shanghai's British and American populations combined. Before the Second Battle of Shanghai, there had been sixty-five Japanese-operated shops along North Sichuan Road. By the battle's official end three months later, the number of Japanese-operated shops had increased tenfold to six hundred and represented ninety percent of all shops along North Sichuan Road.

As the Japanese population and businesses concentrated in the Hongkou district, Chinese residents and businesses moved to other parts of the city. Chinese intellectuals like Xia Mianzun and Zhang Xichen (1889-1969) of Kaiming Press and members of Lu Xun's extended family, who had clustered in the district, came to view the Japanese community as "imperialist." In solidarity with their fellow Chinese, they moved to other parts of Shanghai. Consequently, by the conclusion of the Second Battle of Shanghai, the Hongkou district was predominantly Japanese.

After nine months, the Uchiyamas returned to Shanghai. To their surprise and delight, their house and the bookstore had survived the fighting intact. First, Uchiyama expressed his extreme gratitude to his Chinese and Japanese employees, who had supported each other in protecting and operating the bookstore in his absence. He also thanked the members of the Japanese Special Naval Landing Force brigade who had risked their lives to protect his property.

Then, adopting a Bible verse as his guiding principle, he set about operating the bookstore under the shadow of ever-mounting distrust, hostility, and war: Do not conform yourselves to this age but be transformed by the renewal of your mind, that you may discern the will of God—and know what is good and pleasing and perfect.[4] In this spirit, Uchiyama redoubled his unswerving commitment to conduct all his daily activities toward fostering mutual understanding between the Chinese and Japanese people.

In September 1937, on arrival in Tokyo, Uchiyama was apprehended and detained at the Hisamatsu Police Station. Over four days, authorities questioned his role in Guo Moruo's December 1928 escape from Shanghai to Japan. His interrogator knew that Uchiyama had asked Tsukamoto Makoto, an undercover Kenpeitai operative in Shanghai, to help get Guo out of Shanghai. His interrogator pressed, "I hear you have around six hundred Chinese and Japanese working for you. We know everything, so you better own up. You hid Guo Moruo. You let go of Kuroda. You looked after Kaji Wataru. You fed and paid boat fare for the communists."[5]

Uchiyama replied, "As a Japanese living abroad, I will feed anybody whether they are a communist, a patriot, or a *rōnin*. If he cannot afford to return home, I will lend him the boat fare. I believe this is what I should do as a fellow Japanese. I will be happy to serve my sentence if this is a crime." Finally, the police released Uchiyama without charges.[6]

Kenpeitai officers were among Uchiyama's Japanese customers. Tsukamoto Makoto was one such customer. In his memoir, Tsukamoto recalled Uchiyama and the bookstore:

KALEIDOSCOPE

On the north end of North Sichuan Road is a Japanese bookstore named Uchiyama Bookstore. The owner is called Uchiyama Kanzō. Many Chinese intellectuals as well as Japanese frequent this store. Such figures as Lu Xun and Guo Moruo, in exile in Japan, are among Uchiyama's friends. I stopped by the bookstore quite often because my office was near. Uchiyama would greet me with a loud "come on in."

As I sat across the table from him on a bamboo chair, his wife came out of the kitchen with excellent tea, and our conversation began. His stories were fascinating and valuable in getting to know about China. I learned that he came to China to sell medicine and stayed. From how he talked about China, I could tell how he loved the country from his heart.

One day, Uchiyama told me, "For your body to get used to China, it takes at least a year. So, when I hire a storekeeper at my place, I don't teach him any work for a year. It's a waste otherwise. At my house, Chinese live the same as us; in the morning, we all eat congee from the vendors together."

I felt like he had sensed my frustration with my work and that he was somehow cautioning me.[7]

Between 1938 and 1942, Hayashi Hidesumi served as head of the Shanghai Kenpeitai. With eighteen subordinates, he managed a force of approximately three hundred officers. In his memoir, Hayashi recounts how, because of their connections and language fluency, Chinese *rōnin* were essential sources of local information. Yet he conceded that he was unable to drink socially with them and dubious about the information they provided, and relied instead on Uchiyama:

> I would go to Uchiyama Bookstore rather than listen to what the *rōnin* tell me. There are various books there, so I would purchase a bunch of books, read them, and if I did not understand something, I would ask Uchiyama. Uchiyama was the most reliable of the *rōnin* – if I can call him that. Nonetheless, I am not the type who can go over to his place and introduce myself as Hayashi from the Shanghai Kenpeitai
>
> One day Uchiyama came up to me – I must have been there over an hour browsing through books – he inquired, "Would you care for a cup of tea?" and led me to a small table at the back of the store. I couldn't just drink without saying something, so I asked where he was from. I didn't mention my name, but he already knew and asked, "Where are you from, Mr. Hayashi?"
>
> Since he already knew who I was, I invited him to meet me at a restaurant to get to know him better. He did not show up, so I contacted him and asked why he had not come. He replied that he did not drink.
>
> Again, I invited him to join me at a restaurant. He replied that he would join me. However, no matter from whom the invitation comes, he detests meetings in restaurants. He does not want to repeat the experience. I told him that I felt the same way as him about meeting in restaurants; I did not want to drink with him but only wanted to get to know him.
>
> We became close, and I would go to his house. Uchiyama Kanzō taught me how to view China and treat the Chinese. I told him, "Neither the army nor the Kenpeitai does any good. If you notice something,

let me know. I will do what I can to deal with it." We promised each other that this would be the deal. Uchiyama pledged to tell me everything, and indeed he did come to me several times, yet when the Kenpeitai caught Lu Xun's wife, he did not come to me.

I feel negatively toward merchants. So, Uchiyama does not score very highly as a businessman. Still, I greatly admire him as a person.[8]

Uchiyama openly detested the military, and throughout the war, his view on the outcome remained pessimistic. During the height of the war in the 1940s, some of Uchiyama's Japanese employees were conscripted. It was customary for relatives and friends to stay overnight with the soldier-to-be and, in the morning, see him off to the front. On the contrary, before his employees left for war, Uchiyama held to his pacifist beliefs and did not wish them good luck.

One day in 1943, some employees were leaving the next day to become soldiers. Uchiyama asked them to gather at the back of the store. One of these employees, Yamanaka Katsutarō, recalled Uchiyama's speech:

We are living in an unfortunate time right now. You are going to the war front as soldiers. You will be pointing your guns toward our Chinese friends. Please keep this in mind and make a conscious effort not to shoot. I regret from the bottom of my heart our invasion of China.

When Yamanaka returned from the war front as a low-ranking soldier, he apologized to Uchiyama. Uchiyama replied, "The army is where one commits big worldly sins. Therefore, a person who is an achiever in the army is not good."[9]

As the war progressed, Uchiyama engaged in "debate fights" with fellow Japanese about the war. When they argued that whatever gave advantage to Japan was "right," Uchiyama countered that "just" and "right" were universal concepts that applied to Chinese and Japanese alike.[10] They asked Uchiyama what he thought China would be like after losing the Second Battle of Shanghai to Japan and how he thought the Japanese should treat the Chinese. Uchiyama answered that the Japanese must know about China and that "most importantly, we Japanese must know the Chinese people."[11] He repeatedly warned the Japanese people that China is not easily understood. In his first book of *mandan,* titled *The Ways of a Living China (Ikeru shina no sugata),* published in 1935, he wrote:

> When one says "China," one refers to an enormous place with a four- to five-thousand-year history. When referring to the "Chinese," one refers to four hundred million people—a number beyond imagination."[12] The landmass is about twenty-eight times that of Japan; the languages spoken are so diverse that one cannot communicate with another. It is as if each province is a country and China is the world.[13]

Governmental bodies such as the Ministry of Finance sent researchers to Shanghai to observe recent trends in various sectors and report back to Japan. These researchers worked in China under the auspices of the military and functioned as civilian military personnel. Uchiyama Bookstore customer Okazaki Kaheita 岡崎嘉平太 (1897-1989), who after WWII was among the founders of All Nippon Airways, was one such person. The Bank of Japan sent him to Shanghai to investigate the city's financial sector. Uchiyama lectured Okazaki and others like him: "What the military does is wrong—aren't you guys working for the military?"[14] As a businessman, Uchiyama was happy to gain such people as customers. Even so, he wrote with frustration and disbelief about scholars and critics who toured around for two or three weeks, then wrote about China in Japan's top magazines and newspapers and implored them to remain in China for five or ten years.

One such customer agreed to stay for two years. Uchiyama replied with an additional request: "Try to spend the two years on research and then produce a report at the end of your stay. Please refrain from writing a report immediately upon your arrival in Shanghai." The customer replied, "Of course, that's not possible. If I do not write a report within one month, my boss will judge me as incompetent. The next thing I know, I will lose my job."

Uchiyama countered, "The people who call you incompetent for not immediately producing reports are the incompetent ones. How can they think it is possible to research this country in even one or two years?"[15]

One can almost hear Uchiyama fume, "How dare you trivialize China and its people? They deserve much more than that!" Uchiyama observed that he could understand Chinese people only after living in China for thirty years.[16] He believed that the Japanese who conducted China-related research were impatient, cut corners, and did not comprehend Chinese customs and psychology.

He argued that Chinese day-to-day living customs are highly complex but that most scholars who conduct research on China study only written words and numbers. In contrast, missionaries arriving in Shanghai from abroad spend two years learning Chinese. They begin their mission only when they can deliver sermons in Chinese. Similarly, he argued that Japanese researchers must spend their time and money on travel instead of dining and entertainment to report on China accurately. Much to his extreme disappointment, his recommended *modus operandi* was rarely practiced throughout the Japanese occupation.

To bridge this knowledge gap about China and the Chinese people, Uchiyama transformed himself from a facilitator of the flow of information between Chinese and Japanese intellectuals and activists into a proselytizer for peace between China and Japan. He believed that peace was achievable only if ordinary Japanese actually "knew" China and the Chinese people. He devoted the remainder of his life to activities that supported this endeavor. His bookstore carried a wide variety of Japanese language materials focused on modern China for his Japanese customers. Yet it was through *mandan* talks and essays about China that Uchiyama most effectively reached the Japanese in Shanghai and beyond.

With Lu Xun's death in 1936, Uchiyama lost a dear friend and the bookstore's cultural salon center. Nonetheless, Lu Xun maintained a prominent and frequent role in Uchiyama's *mandan*. By highlighting his connections with Lu Xun and Chinese and Japanese cultural literati, Uchiyama claimed authority over others who wrote and spoke about China. He saw intrinsic depth in Chinese people and their life-risking experiences. Therefore, he took the side of the Chinese people, refusing to let them be trodden upon by those blinded by the "Law of Progress." In his 1941 book *Breezy Talks in Shanghai* (*Shanghai fūgo*), he described his *mandan*:

> During my talks on China, people ask where the stories are written. I reply, some facts are not written in books. Then they say that these may be self-proclaimed truths, to which I have no choice but to respond, "That may be so." The person's face expresses ridicule as if to say, "Your self-proclaimed truth counts for nothing." In China, numerous facts are lying around that have

never been written or printed.[17]

In a typical essay, he describes the love between two people. He then compares it to the relationship between China and Japan:

> I have heard it said that to love a person, you must forget about all the negative aspects of the person you love. I would say that this logic applies when one tries to understand another person. Otherwise, it is difficult to love. Therefore, for China and Japan to genuinely understand and love one another, we must both forget about all the negative aspects of the other.[18]

Uchiyama observed that Chinese culture was expressed in two forms: in writing (文字) and day-to-day life (生活).[19] According to Uchiyama, Japanese Sinologists focused only on written sources and did not observe how the Chinese lived. They looked down on such efforts and believed that research based on written sources was superior to studies based on lived experiences. As a bookstore owner, Uchiyama recognized the value of the written word. Still, he also believed firmly in the value of the spoken word. Because *mandan* are written or spoken, they were Uchiyama's natural choice and preferred communication style. Even in written form, one can easily imagine someone telling the story before an audience.

Between 1933 and 1934, Uchiyama began taking his *mandan* talks beyond the salon and the walls of Uchiyama Bookstore. With Miki's help, he refined his repertoire of stories based on stories he had heard from Lu Xun and on Russian fairy tales recounted in the writings of Leo Tolstoy. Then Uchiyama invited his shop assistants to stay after closing to listen to his stories and make suggestions. After that, he prepared and distributed leaflets inviting children to his Story Time each Sunday night at their Christian or Buddhist school. Story Time expanded from a modest beginning to include young people working in nearby factories and grew to reach five-hundred children weekly. Bookstore customers who worked for Japanese companies were another target audience, and he began to distribute booklets to them. Titled *Mandan*, each booklet contained seventeen stories.

Although he had already earned a "bad name" among some, Uchiyama also told his stories to groups of Japanese military personnel. Executive military officers gave friendly warnings: "Your stories leave a bad sake taste."[20] However, those with real war experiences supported him with comments like, "What he is saying is true."[21] Uchiyama claimed that rather than being told off, there were even times when an executive officer would exclaim, "Damn it, I should have heard this story earlier."[22]

His stories in *The Ways of a Living China* covered a wide range of topics: humor in Chinese daily life, gourmet dining, drinking, beggars and coolies, critiques of the upper-class, dialogues between Chinese people, travels, and Chinese literature. Then in 1937, while he and Miki took refuge in Japan during the Second Battle of Shanghai, Uchiyama gave seventeen talks in ten cities around Japan and fifteen Manchurian cities on the subject, Talking about China. Despite cautionary warnings from the Japanese Embassy, Japanese news agencies established during the occupation, such as *Continental News* (*Tairiku shinpō*),[23] the leading Japanese language newspaper in Shanghai, published his essays. During the 1940s, he began writing for Tokyo-based publications, including the monthly literary magazine *Chūōkōron* and for Kaizōsha's *Tairiku* magazine, a monthly piece titled "Letters from Shanghai."

Two characteristics of Uchiyama's *mandan* stand out first, the Chinese perspectives on how things function in China, and second, a sense of the Chinese's love for their fellow human beings. In his preface to Uchiyama's 1935 book of *mandan*, Lu Xun observed that the Japanese are fond of arriving at conclusions. He accused Japanese sinologists of drawing hasty conclusions about the Chinese without thoroughly researching their subject matter. In contrast, Lu Xun observed that Uchiyama had lived in China for over twenty years, traveled extensively, dealt with people of all social backgrounds, and was qualified to write about China and Chinese people. Lu Xun added that the only negative aspect of Uchiyama's *mandan* was that they tended to speak too fondly of China's positive aspects—a stance Lu Xun disagreed with. However, Lu Xun concluded that it was a good thing that the *mandan* were just casual talk and did not draw conclusions.[24]

Uchiyama argued in his autobiography that the Japanese mistakenly thought China was backward or barbaric. He asserted that he did not intentionally write only positively about China but wanted to introduce aspects of the Chinese unknown in Japan. Uchiyama maintained that he attempted to think like a Chinese while composing each story. Because each *mandan* came from his interpretation of a Chinese perspective, it can seem that he was intentionally portraying the Chinese positively.

Many of Uchiyama's stories aimed to counter and dispel commonly held Japanese stereotypes of Chinese people and their customs. He criticized the tendency of the Japanese to judge the Chinese from the perspective of Japanese customs. He was particularly critical of those in leadership positions whom he accused of leading the rest of the country to believe that barbarians inhabited China. He told of aspects of Chinese society that he considered advanced. For example, he pointed to the Chinese custom of engaging an "intermediary" to solve disagreements between parties. He argued:

> Our scale of measurement differs from the scale held by the Chinese. Therefore, even if we try to

measure using our standards, we will not measure accurately. To measure China, we must use a Chinese measurement scale; otherwise, it is impossible to measure accurately.[25]

Uchiyama noted that the Japanese often criticize Chinese ritualistic behavior—if a Chinese invites you for a meal, then, in return, that person expects a reciprocal invitation. The Japanese assume that such ritual-based obligations define all relationships between Chinese people. Uchiyama disputed the assumption and argued that bureaucrats primarily practice this ritualistic behavior. He observed that there was never the expectation of an equivalent invitation in his relationships with Chinese friends. Then, he observed that the Japanese should be mindful of their ritualistic traditions. Uchiyama referred to the Japanese custom of enclosing a thank-you gift when returning a borrowed item. He quoted Lu Xun, who said if a borrower sent a gift to a Chinese along with a returned item, it would imply that the borrower had not entirely accepted the loan of the borrowed item.

Uchiyama observed that Japanese people maintain that the Chinese people love their money more than their lives. But he contended that everybody desires money—the only difference being that some admit the fact openly. In contrast, others pretend not to like money even though they do. Uchiyama contended that the Chinese easily let go of money in matters of day-to-day humanity, for example, providing ransom when a kidnapping occurs. He illustrated his point with a story: Lu Xun came to the bookstore to pick up a 100 yuan payment for a manuscript. Lu Xun and Uchiyama were chatting when a Chinese lady came into the bookstore. Lu Xun gave her the 100 yuan. Uchiyama asked why he had done this. Lu Xun explained that the woman was trying to free her husband from prison and only had 200 yuan of the 300 yuan she needed to secure his release. Uchiyama countered that he would tell the woman the guards were using her and would not give her the money. Lu Xun refuted Uchiyama's argument. He declared that, according to Chinese custom, when someone who "does not have" asks for something you "have," it is "right" to give what you have.[26]

During the Japanese occupation of Shanghai, Uchiyama organized groups of Chinese and Japanese to engage in conversations to explore why the Chinese and Japanese do not get along. Topics included "Japanese common knowledge of the Chinese" and "Chinese common knowledge of the Japanese." Uchiyama's stories based on these discussions read like ten ways to bad-mouth the Japanese and Chinese:

> The Japanese notion of the Chinese is that they place more importance on money than on lives, are polygamous, steal with no hesitation, are cowardly, and are hedonistic. On the other hand, the Chinese notion of the Japanese is that they use people, look down on the Chinese, are unapproachable, appear well-mannered but are not sincere, and cannot be trusted.[27]
>
> Chinese do not have a sense of nation, are unclean, tell lies, are superstitious, do not have a sense of gratitude, are selfish, and like to gamble. On the other hand, the Japanese are short-tempered, stingy, sinister, cowardly, become fearless when they drink and resort immediately to punching people, appear strict but in reality are not, have a shallow sense of logic, are childish, make grandiose statements which they are unable to support with facts.[28]

Critiquing these views, Uchiyama commented that one could not conclude that all the Chinese behave one way or that all the Japanese behave another way. He invited readers to distinguish between the behavior of the "haves" and the "have-nots" within each society and be mindful of how current attitudes have changed over time. Uchiyama cautioned his audience that the perspective from which Japanese and Chinese people view a particular concept may differ. Occasionally, he fully agreed or disagreed with one group's judgments of the other. However, he often concluded that there were only differences in degree between the two cultures.

Despite Uchiyama's tendency to portray the Chinese positively, he did not pretend that they were utterly unblemished. After the end of the war, many disarmed Japanese soldiers had walked hundreds of miles across China to reach evacuation points. On their return to Japan, the soldiers reported that they had survived thanks to the Chinese people who generously fed them. Uchiyama questioned whether this was an accurate interpretation of Chinese generosity. He cautioned that in the minds of ordinary Chinese, soldiers of any kind are a threat of robbery or worse. He continued, "one must know that there is an old saying in China—if you do not eat for a day, you starve, if you do not eat for two days, you rob, and if you do not eat for three days, you kill."[29]

Uchiyama knew the dangers of rhetoric and was critical of the Japanese, who advocated Sino-Japanese friendship and co-existence out of political correctness or naivety but without genuine respect for the Chinese people. He noted that newspapers admonished the Japanese, "Let us stop using Shina and call it China." He agreed but added that if we Japanese do not change our attitudes, it makes no difference whether we use the word "Shina" or "China."

Uchiyama pointed to his friend B as an example of action

based on genuine care rather than rhetoric. A few months after the Manchurian Incident that sparked skirmishes between Chinese and Japanese soldiers in Manchuria, his friend B frequently went to a Shanghai shrine on behalf of Japanese soldiers, even though he did not have a son or a brother fighting on the front. One day, B came to the bookstore with a stack of five hundred postcards addressed to the families of Japanese soldiers, letting them know the whereabouts of their loved ones. He planned to send one thousand more such postcards. Though numerous groups and organizations organized volunteers to console families who had lost loved ones in war, Uchiyama was impressed that B had made a personal choice to devote himself to this effort.

Uchiyama noted that in both Chinese and Japanese, the ideogram for "good" 善, "beautiful" 美, and "morality, righteousness, justice, and honor" 義 all contain the ideogram for "sheep" 羊. He urged his Japanese audience to emulate sheep that gather in large flocks but do not fight. Uchiyama took the biblical admonition, "love your neighbor as yourself," as his guide. Through the medium of his *mandan,* he aimed to influence his Japanese audience to view all the world's people as neighbors deserving of their love—especially their closest neighbors, the Chinese.

On January 3, 1932, just a few weeks before the January 28 Incident, Uchiyama's neighbor, and bookstore regular Sakamoto Yoshitaka, president of the Shanghai Japanese YMCA and a professor at EACCA, invited Uchiyama to lunch with a group of prominent Japanese Christians. The group included Nitobe Inazō (Chapter 3), who was among the founders in 1925 of the Institute of Pacific Relations (IPR),[30] Maeda Tamon 前田多門 (1884-1962), a disciple of Nitobe and IPR member, and journalist and bookstore customer Matsumoto Shigeharu 松本重治 (1889-1989). A special edition of the newspaper had just announced the Japanese Army's occupation of Jinzhou (in Manchuria). Nitobe was sitting off to the side reading the newspaper when Uchiyama overheard him mumble to himself, "In the end, the army will lead Japan into defeat."[31]

These men were spokesmen to the international community on behalf of others in Japan who shared their views. People such as these men came together to form the three organizations that most actively promoted international peace during the Second Sino-Japanese War and WWII: the Fellowship of Reconciliation (FOR), founded in 1926 by Nitobe Inazō and Kagawa Toyohiko; the League of Nations Association of Japan (LNAJ) also founded in 1926 by Nitobe Inazō and Kagawa Toyohiko; and the Peace Federation, founded in 1932 by Kagawa Toyohiko to address the international crisis precipitated by the Manchurian and Shanghai Incidents. Since 1920, when Uchiyama had selected Kagawa Toyohiko to participate in the Shanghai Japanese YMCA Summer Lecture Series, the two had maintained their friendship. Uchiyama's friendship with Kagawa linked him with all three of Japan's peace-related organizations.

A month after the January 28th Incident, in the city of Matsuyama, where he was giving a talk, Nitobe stated, "our country will be destroyed by the military clique or the Communist Party. If asked which I fear, I have to say; currently, it is the military." Consequently, the authorities forced him to apologize to the military and effectively silenced him for the duration of the war. Similarly, Kagawa published a magazine article appealing to an ethic higher than war to resolve the conflicts between Japan and China. As a result, police confiscated and destroyed the entire edition. Nevertheless, in contrast to Nitobe, because Kagawa emphasized the unarguable connection between peace and economics, authorities allowed him to continue carrying out his peace-related activities throughout the war.[32]

KALEIDOSCOPE

Under the Empire of Japan's Public Security Preservation Laws enacted between 1894 and 1925, activists at odds with the Japanese state risked harsh punishment. Before the 1930s, the Japanese Civilian Secret Police Force (Tokkō) primarily suppressed the spread of communism. In the 1930s, Ōmoto, a Shintō sect founded in 1892, gained followers in Japan and threatened State Shintoism. Under its 1935 Report on Religious Movements, Tokkō [33] designated both Ōmoto and Christianity threats to State Shintoism and extended suppression to both. A section of the report titled, Attitudes of the Christian World during the time of the Second Sino-Japanese War, describes the Christian vision of peace:

> Political tendencies of the nation-state do not control Christians, but persistently and with great pride, they hold to their vision of peace. Not only do they possess thoughts that are separate from the thought of the nation-state, but they openly act and speak as unpatriotic citizens.[34]

Nevertheless, despite seemingly overwhelming odds against the success of their activities, an international network of Japan-based socialist and Christian groups maintained their efforts to reconcile with China and work toward peace. This network was the root out of which Japanese post-WWII peace movements grew.

Endnotes:
1 Also known as the War of Resistance against Japan
2 Nakamura Shintarō, *Sonbun kara Ozaki Hotsumi e* (Tokyo: Nitchū, Shuppan, 1975), 206.
3 Kaji Wataru, *Shanhai senki no naka*, (Tokyo: Tōho Publications, 1975), 212.
4 Uchiyama Kanzō, *Kakōroku*, 62. *The Bible.* King James version, Romans 12:2.
5 Kuroda was likely Aoyama Kazuo, who was also known as Kuroda Zenji, a member of the JCP and leading member of Japan's antiwar movement.
6 Ozawa Masamoto, *Uchiyama Kanzō den: Nitchū yūkō ni tsukushita idai na shomin*, 154-155.
7 Tsukamoto Makoto, *Aru jōhō shōkō no kiroku* (Tokyo: Chūō Kōronsha, 1998), 137-138.
8 Kidonikki Kenkyū-kai. *Hayashi Hidesumi shi danwa sokkiroku III.* (Tokyo: Nihon Kindai Shiryō Kenkyū kai, 1974-1980), 83-86.
9 Yoshida Hiroji, *Rojin no tomo Uchiyama Kanzō no shōzō*, 231-232.
10 Uchiyama Kanzō, *Kakōroku*, 88.
11 Uchiyama Kanzō, *Shanhai mango* (Tokyo: Kaizōsha 1941), 141.
12 Uchiyama Kanzō, *Shanhai mango*, 27.
13 Uchiyama Kanzō, *Chūgoku: Rinpō chiri* (Tokyo: Tamagawa Daigaku Shuppanbu), 117.
14 Okazaki Kaheita,"Intabyū chūgoku to chūgokujin," *Kikan Uchiyama* 2 (1983): 2.
15 Uchiyama Kanzō, *Shanhai mango*, 230.
16 Kataoka Kazuo. "Nakanishi Kanji zuisōki: Uchiyama Kanzō san no omoide." *Okayama to chūgoku* (2008).
17 Uchiyama Kanzō, *Shanhai mango*, 298-299.
18 Uchiyama Kanzō, *Kakōroku*, 334-335.
19 Uchiyama Kanzō, *Shanhai yawa* (Tokyo: Kaizōsha, 1940), 51.
20 Uchiyama Kanzō, *Kakōroku*, 292.

21 Uchiyama Kanzō, *Kakōroku*, 249.
22 Uchiyama Kanzō, *Kakōroku*, 292.
23 Continental News was a Japanese-language newspaper published in Shanghai during the Japanese occupation.
24 Uchiyama Kanzō, *Ikeru shina no sugata: Uchisan manbun* (Tokyo: Gakugei Shoin, 1935), 1-6.
25 Uchiyama Kanzō, *Shanhai mango*, 30.
26 Uchiyama Kanzō, *Rojin no omoide*, 74.
27 Uchiyama Kanzō, *Chūgokujin no seikatsu fūkei: Uchiyama Kanzō mango* (Tokyo: Tōhō Shuppan, 1979), 66.
28 Uchiyama Kanzō, *Ryanpentō* (Tokyo: Kangensha, 1953), 21.
29 Uchiyama Kanzō, *Ryanpentō*, 39.
30 Institute of Pacific Relations (IPR) was an international NGO. It provided a forum in which nations of the Pacific Rim came together to discuss problems and relations. IPR played a major role in the emergence of contemporary Asian and Pacific Studies in Western universities and institutions. It was established in 1925 and dissolved in 1960.
31 Uchiyama Kanzō, *Kakōroku*, 186.
32 Japan's post-war cooperative sector, one of the largest globally, grew out of Kagawa's peace-related work through his evangelical and cooperative Kingdom of God Movement.
33 Tokubetsu Kōtō Keisatsu (特別高等警察, Special Higher Police), also known as the Tokkō (特高), established in 1911, to handle high-level policing, criminal investigation, counterespionage, and to control political groups and ideologies deemed a threat to public order of the Empire of Japan. Tokkō was the civilian counterpart to the Kenpeitai, the military police force of the Imperial Japanese Army and Navy.
34 Dōshisha daigaku jinbun kagaku kenkyūjo kirisuto kyō shakai mondai kenkyū. *Senjika no kirisuto kyō undō 1: Tokkō shiryō ni yoru shōwa 11 kara.* (Tokyo: Shinkyo Shuppansha, 1972).

SEVENTH TURN OF THE KALEIDOSCOPE

JAPAN-CHINA FRIENDSHIP ASSOCIATION (1945-1959)

ON JANUARY 9, 1945, Kanzō and Miki Uchiyama celebrated their thirtieth wedding anniversary. That day Kanzō wrote to Pastor Makino Toraji, who in 1913 had inspired him to go to China and three years later had introduced him to Miki. January 11 was Uchiyama's 60th birthday—his *kanreki* marking rebirth into a new life.[1] He, Miki, and their friends celebrated in the traditional Japanese way by eating *sekihan*, made from glutinous rice and *azuki* beans.[2] Just two days later, on January 13, Miki passed away. Overnight, Uchiyama and a few close friends, including Tsukamoto Suketarō, kept vigil with Miki's body before the next day's funeral. As they sat with Miki's remains, Uchiyama revealed her past as an entertainer in Kyoto's *Gion* entertainment district for the first time.

Uchiyama spent ten days after Miki's funeral alone at home, grieving and pondering the next phase of his life. Tsukamoto sensed how devastated Miki's death had left his dear friend. Hoping to bring Kanzō "back to life," Tsukamoto suggested that Uchiyama build a double grave monument where he would rejoin Miki one day. Tsukamoto proposed a stone memorial monument with a bridge and an open book in front. On the book's pages, he suggested Uchiyama have this epitaph inscribed:[3]

> Through a bookstore, a bridge to cultural exchange,
> In life becoming China's friends,
> Like all other Japanese businesses In death becoming China's soil,
> Ah — such a couple.
>
> (Translation by John Darwin Van Fleet. Used with permission.)

During those ten days of contemplation, Uchiyama did not determine his future. Nonetheless, he carried on as a cultural mediator, and his future path began to open before him.

In Japan, just a few months later, on August 15, 1945, after the atomic bombing of Hiroshima and Nagasaki, Emperor Hirohito announced Japan's surrender in a carefully scripted radio address to the nation.[4] The Allies designated U.S. Army General Douglas MacArthur (1880-1964) as Supreme Commander of the Allied Powers (SCAP) to oversee the occupation of Japan. In September, the occupation force requisitioned the Dai-ichi Seimei headquarters building in Tokyo to serve as General Headquarters (GHQ). It would house the staff of several hundred U.S. government civil servants and military personnel to manage the Allied occupation.

According to the text of the Initial Post-Surrender Policy for Japan, the primary objective of the occupation was to prepare

Japan for re-entry into the international community as a peaceful democracy and "to ensure that Japan does not again become a menace to the United States or the peace and security of the world." Furthermore, the Policy stipulated that the objectives would be achieved through political, economic, and social reform of fundamental Japanese values, "by means which will best serve to make the results permanent" and "through the education of the individuals to new values, hoping that as they learn they will change their laws and institutions to conform to purposes which we wish to promote."

Many among the samurai class of the shogunate period who became Meiji period reformers believed that Christian principles were essential to modern Japan. In 1875, Christian educator Niijima Jō founded Dōshisha English School, which would evolve into Dōshisha University. Niijima believed that Christian education would save the souls of the Japanese people and save the nation and the state from what he viewed as its moral and social stagnation. Furthermore, Niijima believed that the responsibility to "redeem" Japan from its past lay in the hands of its Christian leaders. Therefore, he thought that those educated at Dōshisha University should form the core of Japan's future leaders.

Correspondingly, among Meiji and Taishō leaders of government, business, and the peace movements, many held Christian-inspired values based on concepts of humanitarianism and peace. Moreover, SCAP intended that the Japanese undertake reform of their society. Japanese Christians, therefore, came to play a pivotal role in shaping postwar Japan. Among those Christians were several men with links reaching back to Niijima Jō and Dōshisha University.

On August 17, 1945, as SCAP was establishing the occupation, Emperor Hirohito appointed Prince Higashikuni Naruhiko 東久邇宮稔彦王 (1887-1990) as Prime Minister following the resignation that day of Suzuki Kantarō 鈴木貫太郎 (1868-1948), who had served since April 7, 1945. At the same time, the Emperor appointed Prince Konoe Fumimaro 近衞文麿 (1891-1945) as Minister of State. A few days later, General MacArthur named Quaker peace activist Kagawa Toyohiko as Special Advisor to Prime Minister Higashikuni. In this role, Kagawa, a longtime friend of Uchiyama Kanzō, was the first private Japanese citizen to meet with General MacArthur. In addition, Kagawa had toured widely in the USA during the war and published extensively in English. Consequently, he had become one of the best-known Japanese Christians in the English-speaking world.

In an open letter to General MacArthur dated September 2, Kagawa asserted that Japan would best achieve democratization by retaining the imperial system.[5] As Special Advisor, Kagawa drafted public statements for Prime Minister Konoe Fumimaro, including arguments defending Japan's imperial system. On September 5, Higashikuni delivered a policy speech reported worldwide. It included a compelling phrase crafted by Kagawa: "One hundred million, all bearing guilt." In the speech, Higashikuni called on the Japanese people to collectively repent as the first step in their country's reconstruction and unification.[6]

Through William Merrell Vories (1880-1964), a lifelong devotee of Christian missionary work, Konoe facilitated the delivery of a "Declaration from the Emperor" to General MacArthur. Vories devised wording that he deemed MacArthur would accept as "worth more than anything else in restoring full confidence in Japan." Lieutenant Barlett, the son of a missionary family, was an aid to General MacArthur. Through Dōshisha University connections, Vories arranged to meet Barlett at GHQ on September 10 and hand-delivered the Declaration.[7] Through Barlett, Vories communicated Konoe's defense to General MacArthur: Emperor Hirohito had favored ending the war. However, the military government had concealed the truth about the war from him.

While Emperor Hirohito's appointed Prime Minister Higashikuni and Minister of State Konoe, to the 54-day long Higashikuni cabinet (August 17 – October 9, 1945), SCAP oversaw the selection of all other cabinet members; all sympathetic to reforming postwar Japanese society. SCAP deemed the Ministry of Education the "central organ of government through which the rulers of Imperial Japan had carried out the indoctrination of the Japanese people with the tenets of militarism, ultranationalism, and State Shintoism"[8] Therefore, SCAP prioritized reform of the Ministry of Education and swiftly named liberal Christian thinker Maeda Tamon as Minister. Maeda served in the cabinets of both Higashikuni and of Higashikuni's successor, Shidehara Kijūrō 幣原 喜重郎 (October 9, 1945 – May 22, 1946). Maeda was a disciple of peace activist Nitobe Inazō who the state had silenced during the war for expressing his pessimistic view of the military. Prime Minister Yoshida Shigeru 吉田茂 (May 22, 1946 – May 24, 1947) succeeded Shidehara. He selected Catholic jurist Tanaka Kōtarō 田中耕太郎 (1890-1974) as Minister of Education in his cabinet (May 22, 1946 – May 24, 1947). Along with Uchiyama Kanzō and many others, Tanaka was a disciple of pacifist and Japan Non-Church Movement founder Uchimura Kanzō. In the 1947 election, Tanaka won a seat in the House of Councilors, where he was among signatories of the 1947 Constitution and instrumental in drafting the postwar Basic Education Law.[9] In 1950, he resigned his seat in the Diet to become Chief Justice of Japan.

Elected under the new Constitution, Diet members named socialist-Christian Katayama Tetsu 片山哲 (1887-1978) as Prime Minister—a disciple of Abe Isō, the father of Japan's Christian-socialist movement. Katayama chose Morito Tatsuo 森戸辰男

KALEIDOSCOPE

(1888-1984) as Minister of Education. Morito was a Dōshisha graduate, a pioneer of the Christian-socialist movement, and a disciple of prominent pacifist Nitobe Inazō. Despite the Katayama cabinet's short duration (May 24, 1947 — March 10, 1948), the Diet enacted a wide range of progressive social reforms under its leadership.[10]

When Japan surrendered to Allied Forces on August 15, 1945, all but one of Shanghai's Japanese-owned shops closed. However, the Uchiyama Bookstore remained open until October 23, when Chinese government authorities officially requisitioned it. Uchiyama estimated that his stock was worth 2.5 billion yuan[11] (Uchiyama referred to *fabi yuan* as *"yuan"*[12]). That day Uchiyama's niece, who was one of his shop assistants, recalled:

> The authorities closed all the bookstore's doors and windows. But when I carefully looked around, the bathroom window was open. So, I suggested to *laoban* (Uchiyama) that he go through that window and take out the expensive books. *Laoban,* however, shook his head and told me off. "Let's not do that. I don't want to be told later by the Chinese that we didn't have any good books. And your idea to do such a thing is the worst."[13]

Uchiyama's fellow Japanese elected him to lead the Mutual Aid Association, Shanghai's Japanese residents' group. The group worked with local Chinese government officials on their behalf to access food, housing, and other necessities as they awaited repatriation to Japan. During this time, Uchiyama held children's storytimes and gave instructional talks on actions required of each district in which Japanese people lived. At the same time, to promote trade and cultural exchange, the Chinese government created the East Asia Association (Atōkyōkai). Uchiyama was among thirty Japanese who volunteered to contribute skills to the cause. Then at the request of former Chinese customers who had studied in Japan, he collected books for the Association's library.

Like all other Japanese businesses in China at the end of the war, *Continental News* (*Tairiku shinpō*), the leading Japanese language newspaper in Shanghai during the occupation, had ceased publication. However, *Reformation Daily* (*Kaizō nippō*), a new Nationalist government-controlled Japanese language newspaper, began publication in October 1945. The newspaper was part of the ROC's "thought reform" program. The newspaper dedicated a section to stories by Japanese residents expressing their viewpoints on issues of the day, including Japanese war crimes and problems with their upcoming repatriation to Japan. Not surprisingly, Uchiyama contributed a piece and titled it "The Concept of Superiority."

After Japan's surrender, the Chinese government required all Japanese nationals residing in Shanghai, including soldiers, to live in one of four residential areas designated for the Japanese. In April 1946, Uchiyama moved from Qianaili to Yifengli 義豊里 off Wusong Road into the same house where he and Miki had begun their life together in Shanghai thirty years before. Housing in the designated areas was insufficient to accommodate all those required to relocate, so more than one family occupied most houses. Uchiyama shared a small house with seven people, including his adopted daughter Nishibayashi Sumi 西林壽美[14] and two of her family members, and his friend Tsukamoto Suketarō and three of Tsukamoto's family members.

Even under such difficult circumstances, Uchiyama maintained his focus on nurturing Sino-Japanese relations. For example, to commemorate the death of Lu Xun ten years earlier, Uchiyama and Shimada Masao assisted in organizing an exhibition of works by woodcut artist disciples of Lu Xun. The exhibition titled *Woodcuts of Wartime China* took place in Shanghai from September 18 through October 3, 1946. That December, Kaiming Press published images of the pieces in a book titled *Woodcuts of Wartime China: 1937-1945*. Then at the end of 1946, Uchiyama contacted his brother Kakichi and asked him to organize an exhibition in Tokyo of woodcuts that had appeared in the book.

Postwar inflation in Shanghai skyrocketed. Forced to move from single-family homes into temporary multiple-family households in designated areas, the Japanese sold whatever they could for money to buy food. Furthermore, the entire Japanese community would soon be returning to Japan. Each person would be allowed to take a limited amount of money and a few goods: 1,000 Japanese *yen*, 30 kg of clothing, a futon and blanket, one set of kitchenware, and whatever else one could carry. This situation prompted the Japanese to open street stalls, many along Shanyin Road, and sell their possessions to Chinese customers.

With the appropriation of his bookstore, Uchiyama had lost all its books and had little to sell. Dr. Sudō, Lu Xun's family doctor and one of the bookstore's most loyal customers, came to Uchiyama's rescue and donated his book collection. Sudō's three-story-plus-attic house was filled from top to bottom with books, many purchased at Uchiyama Bookstore and few of which he could take to Japan. With Sudō's collection as its foundation, books purchased from other Japanese, and assistance with monthly expenses from the bookstore's longest-serving employee Wang Horian, in February 1947, Uchiyama opened Yijian Bookstore 一間書店, a second-hand bookshop in his house.

One day Uchiyama's friend, artist Feng Zikai, dropped in looking for the collected works of Japanese novelist Natsume

Sōseki 夏目漱石 (1867-1916). Uchiyama had seventeen of the twenty-volume set in stock and sold them to Feng for 170,000 *yuan*. Feng paid, commented on the low price, and asked Uchiyama to send any additional volumes he received. Feng added, "Don't go back. Stay in Shanghai. You don't need to worry about making a living; you have many friends here. Rest assured that things will be fine." Upon receiving one of the missing volumes, Uchiyama sent it to Feng along with a letter and bill for 10,000 *yuan*. A few days later, Uchiyama received a money order and a letter from Feng, "I am sending 100,000 *yuan* because 10,000 *yuan* is too cheap." Uchiyama was initially puzzled but realized that Feng wanted to assist in his struggle to make ends meet.[15]

In mid-November 1947, before the ROC authorities could arrest him, Guo Moruo fled to Hong Kong. Before leaving Shanghai, he and his wife stopped by Uchiyama's house for a visit. Uchiyama was not at home, so Guo left a few magazines and a small photo. On the morning of December 6, Uchiyama received a letter from Guo sent from Hong Kong, "I have arrived safely, so please be assured. Thank you for all that you did in Shanghai for me. If we're both alive, in a few years, we'll probably have a chance to have dinner and a laugh together."[16] Later that same day, an armed government security force occupied the lane where Uchiyama lived. Uchiyama writes of the experience:

> Tsukamoto and I were trapped after we headed up to the second floor of a high school classroom next to the Mutual Aid Association for Japanese residents. Thirty-three of us were rounded up. I was the much-rumored "big shot" among the group. We were ordered to leave the country by 5:00 AM the next day.[17]

Later Tsukamoto Suketarō surmised that the authorities deported

Uchiyama because of his connection with Guo Moruo, a known CPC member.

With Miki's death, the confiscation of his bookstore, and deportation from China, Uchiyama lost his treasured life partner and his beloved Shanghai community. Nonetheless, he remained determined to pursue his work on behalf of Sino-Japanese cultural exchange. After thirty years, Uchiyama embarked on life anew in postwar Japan; thus, continuing to deserve the epitaph already inscribed on his tombstone.

His destination was Tokyo and the home of his brother Uchiyama Kakichi and Kakichi's wife Matsumo. They lived in the Jinbōchō bookstore district near the Tokyo branch of Uchiyama Bookstore, which Kakichi established in 1935 at Kanzō's suggestion. From then on, promoting Sino-Japanese cultural relations became Uchiyama Kanzō's duty, obligation, and full-time job.

For a short time, Kanzō helped at the bookstore. Friends heard that he was in Tokyo and frequently came to visit. It was as if Shanghai Uchiyama Bookstore had been reborn in Tokyo. However, early in 1948, Kobayashi Isamu 小林勇 (1903-1981), a prolific writer who published with Iwanami Shoten, invited Kanzō to Nagano Prefecture to give a series of talks. Recognizing an opportunity to renew his efforts to foster Sino-Japanese friendship, Uchiyama accepted the invitation and set off on a seventeen-month-long journey across Japan. He called these and his other *mandan* tours "pilgrimages" (*angya*). Given the times and the *mandans*' themes of peace, friendship, trade, and reconciliation, and Uchiyama's commitment to strengthening ties between two countries ravaged by war, his *mandan* tours were indeed like the efforts of an itinerant monk. During his 1948 "pilgrimage," Uchiyama delivered approximately eight hundred talks to audiences ranging from 50 to 1,700.

From his new base in Tokyo, Uchiyama continued to promote Sino-Japanese friendship and efforts to humanize the Chinese in the minds of the Japanese. Through both speaking and publishing, he called out negative attitudes of the Japanese toward the Chinese. He began publishing *mandan* in local media and, in 1948, published his first book in Japanese. The title, *Friends with the Same Blood Running Through* (*Onaji chi no nagare no tomo yo*), combined his Christian-based ideal of common humanity and his Pan-Asian perspective expressed by the phrase *dōbun dōshu* (same script, same kind).

Uchiyama cautioned his Japanese audience not to measure China by Western standards and then conclude that Chinese civilization was a failure. Based on thirty-four years in China interacting with Chinese people, he believed that the Chinese hold cultural norms based on collective wisdom acquired through centuries of experience. Provocatively, Uchiyama urged his Japanese audience to question the cultural norms against which they judged China and explore other standards against which to compare the two cultures. He argued, for example, that in the West, the word "trust" often refers to a property interest, such as real estate or money. In contrast, "trust," as in "trustworthy," is secondary. The Japanese, he contended, "are abandoning the spiritual trust in personal character and instead, basing trust in material assets." Uchiyama argued that East Asian culture should abandon the Western prioritization of trust in material things and return to trust in matters of the spirit."[18]

"China as an adult and Japan as a child" was a recurring theme in Uchiyama's postwar stories. Historically, Japan looked up to China as the teacher, the source of wisdom, and the fountain of culture and knowledge, so the metaphor was familiar. Until the mid-19th century, China stood at the center of a tributary system in which Japan paid homage to the Chinese emperor. In his 1955 book written in Japanese, *China's Past and Present* (*Heikin yūsen: Chūgoku no konjaku*), Uchiyama noted that Japan's history is only half as long as China's. Consequently, he maintained that Japanese culture is still emerging and remains "half a culture." To illustrate, he compared two aspects of culture, which he called "format culture" and "practical culture." He argued that Japanese culture emphasizes "format" over the "practical." To illustrate, he pointed to the sudden postwar spread of the trappings of Christmas across Japan. He observed that the Japanese followed the example of their American occupiers and adopted the "form" of Christmas devoid of its original meaning.[19]

Continuing his comparative analysis, Uchiyama contrasted Japanese "simplicity" and Chinese "complexity" with day-to-day life examples. For example, when asked about "inflation," he contended that a Japanese would answer that inflation was difficult because things become more expensive. On the other hand, a Chinese would explain that things became more costly as the value of the money decreased. Furthermore, Uchiyama observed that while the Japanese grasp the concept of cause and effect, they fail to see the causal relationship among events of daily life. They also fail to see the causal relationship among historical events. Because the Japanese have not cultivated the ability to grasp the connection between complex matters, he called them "simple-minded."[20] Finally, to further demonstrate the relative cultural maturity between China and Japan, Uchiyama described the difference between the two countries' prewar decisions. He observed that the Empire of Japan led the entire country into war under a group of like-minded leaders. On the other hand, Uchiyama observed that China's leaders practiced a balanced approach to decision-making built on a foundation of collective wisdom acquired through centuries of experience that minimized dangerous risk-taking, and they did not gamble with the land and people of China.[21]

Uchiyama described problem-solving through arbitration as another example of China's highly developed cultural maturity relative to Japan. Instead of keeping disagreements inside the house as the Japanese do, he described how the Chinese take disagreements out onto the street for arbitration by a crowd of diverse people. The difference in social status between the arguing parties does not sway the group's collective judgment. Hence, a coolie and his employer or a servant and his master have equal opportunities to state their cases and be heard and judged by the crowd.[22]

Alongside his *mandan* activities, Uchiyama contributed 250 pages on China to an encyclopedia for school-age children. His topics ranged from governance to geography, weather, history, transportation, communication, industry, inhabitants, customs, statistics, maps, and photos. He opened his section by stating that humans are imperfect and do things based on wrong thinking. He noted that the Japanese make mistakes and recently had made big mistakes; one of their greatest mistakes had been their disrespectful treatment of China and the Chinese people.

In the encyclopedia, Uchiyama described two recently developed habits of the Japanese that he judged to be unwise — an addiction to things Western and gazing down in disdain upon Chinese ways and looking upon China as weak and backward and left behind by modern civilization. He acknowledged the numerous ways in which ideas from the West had benefited the East but advised his young readers to learn from the wisdom of the Chinese people too. Quoting Lu Xun, Uchiyama encouraged readers to acknowledge their tendency to overly admire the West and under-appreciate China:

The Japanese should be the ones who know China the best because they have used the same written characters as the

Chinese for centuries. However, the truth of the matter is that the Japanese are the ones who know China the least. The Japanese study China a great deal, but they base their studies of China on Western research and writing. They do not research China. Therefore, Western studies of China are "off the point." If the Japanese place importance on studies of China that are "off the point," then studies of China by the Japanese end up the same way — "off the point."[23]

Affirming Lu Xun's advice, he appealed to young readers: "Use your ability to read the Chinese language and take China studies into your own Asian hands."

In his stories, Uchiyama criticized an attitude he observed among the Japanese during the war: "Make do — just get things done efficiently." He argued that there are consequences when an individual or a nation "goes with the flow" from one situation to the next without considering the search for truth. He likened the result of Japan's behavior during the war years toward both its enemies and its people to a fall from a high mountain top into a bottomless abyss. Rather than fully experiencing the suffering of the precipitous fall, Uchiyama contended that Japan and its people had only half-heartedly accepted responsibility for their actions during the war. Thus, Japan denied itself the opportunity to confront its shame, grieve for its actions, and heal from its suffering. He compared the numerous "National Shame Days" observed in China to Japan's failure to acknowledge its own "shame days."[24]

In the same vein, he called out the citizens of Hiroshima and Nagasaki. After the bombing of their cities, rather than speak out against the use of nuclear weapons, they remained silent. He criticized their lack of principles and morality. Uchiyama detested this "make do" attitude. He urged readers to heed the warning of Christian teacher Paul to Christians subjected by

Roman authorities to persecution and even death for their faith, "Do not grow slack in zeal. Be fervent in spirit."[25]

In 1950, Uchiyama married Kato Masano from Moji, a port city connected with Nagasaki by train. Years before, Miki had managed a bookstore in Nagasaki while in Japan recovering from a heart ailment. During his travels in Japan between 1938 and 1941, Uchiyama made frequent trips to Nagasaki to see Miki and give *mandan* talks in the surrounding towns. According to Uchiyama's adopted daughter Nishibayashi Sumi, Masano and Miki met at Moji Church when Uchiyama spoke there.[26] Miki and Masano had formed a special connection because both were former women of the entertainment district.[27] Later, when Masano attempted suicide, Miki ran to Masano's house and saved her. After their marriage, Uchiyama and Masano moved into a place in the Kyōdō kita area of Tokyo's Setagaya ward. After that, they joined the United Church of Christ near their home, where Murata Masasuke, an old and dear friend of Uchiyama from Shanghai, was the pastor.

Before Uchiyama settled down in Tokyo after his speaking tour, the "Shanghai Group" had begun preparing to establish the Japan-China Friendship Association (JCFA). The group, comprised almost entirely of Uchiyama's friends from Shanghai and a few like-minded overseas Chinese, met in the Overseas Chinese Association (*Kakyō Sōkai*) office near Tokyo Station.[28] On October 1, 1950, exactly one year after the PRC, its founders officially launched JCFA as a "friendship movement" with Uchiyama Kanzō as chairman. In the spirit of Uchiyama Bookstore, JCFA leaders and members encompassed all classes of Japanese and Chinese peoples, including Chinese residing in Japan. From its beginning, JCFA was undeterred by anti-communist pressure and called on the Japanese government to prioritize the normalization of diplomatic relations with the PRC.

Although Uchiyama Bookstore in Shanghai was not the predecessor of JCFA, the Association's founding aims overlapped with those of the bookstore. It grew out of Uchiyama's beliefs expressed in his *mandan* talks, published works, and the Sino-Japanese networks developed during his thirty-four years in China. Thus, the founding aims of JCFA were to:

- Deeply examine and correct mistaken notions of China held by the Japanese.
- Build mutual understanding and cooperation between the people of China and Japan by promoting cultural exchange, including woodblock prints, film, theater, art, music, photography, and translation.
- Promote trade between China and Japan to build the economies and improve the livelihoods of the peoples of both countries.
- Cooperate with other peace movement organizations to contribute to world peace by ensuring mutual security through Sino-Japanese cooperative friendship.[29]

The first aim of JCFA, to examine and correct mistaken notions of China held by the Japanese, incorporates the concept of "decolonization" — the process of undoing colonialism. To this day, JCFA continues its focus on decolonization and raises awareness of Japanese atrocities in China. Soon after its founding, JCFA embarked on two decolonization initiatives: recovery and return to China of the remains of Chinese victims of Japanese forced labor and repatriation of Japanese people left behind in China.

Starting in 1949 with Hanaoka Mine in Akita Prefecture, the Overseas Chinese Association began collecting the remains of deceased Chinese forced laborers. By November 1950, the remains of more than 400 Chinese had been collected and moved to a temple in Tokyo's Asakusa district. In November 1950, the bulletin of JCFA began publishing a list of the names of Japanese missing in China. In December 1952, the Japanese Red Cross Society and JCFA's Peace Liaison Committee (Heiwa renrakukai) worked with Liao Chengzhi 廖承志 (1908-1983) of the Red Cross Society of China to negotiate repatriation. Between March 1953 and July 1958, 35,000 Japanese displaced in China returned to Japan.[30]

Then in June 1956, the PRC, with the assistance of the Peace Liaison Committee, began the handover of former Japanese soldiers held at the Fushun War Criminals Management Center in China's Liaoning province to the Red Cross Society of China for repatriation to Japan.[31] After they surrendered in 1945, the Chinese held the group for more than five years. The Chinese subjected the former soldiers to physical labor, the process of admitting past wrongdoings, and finally to an eight-month "apology movement" during which authorities required each detainee to write, reflect upon, and edit his testimony.

A group of returnees formed the Association of Japanese Repatriates from China (*Chūkiren*) in 1957. With the primary aim of "apology" through active admittance of wrongdoing, *Chūkiren* became one of Japan's strongest postwar peace advocates. Film director Matsui Minoru 松井稔 (1947-) created his 2001 documentary *Japanese Devils: Confessions of Imperial Army Soldiers from Japan's War against China*, based on interviews with fourteen *Chūkiren* members. During the interviews, Matsui's informants, all in their eighties, recounted rape, massacres, bio-experiments, and cannibalism that they and others in the Imperial Japanese Army committed between 1931 and 1945.[32]

The Hanaoka Mine Project was the other of JCFA's early

decolonization projects. The project recounted the Chinese and Korean laborers' uprising against Japanese supervisors that ended on June 30, 1945, with the massacre of 418 of the mine's 986 forced laborers. Its JCFA creators conceived the story of atonement in the form of "paper drama" (*kamishibai*), in which slideshow-like, illustrated storyboards depict the story. In 1951, JCFA published a book titled *Hanaoka Story*. Woodcut prints graphically depict the conditions under which *Hanaoka* laborers suffered. The choice of the woodcut form of political protest art to illustrate the book was fitting. Significantly, Chinese woodcut artists directly influenced the Japanese artists who created the woodcuts that illustrated *Hanaoka Story*.

In Shanghai before his 1947 deportation, Uchiyama had already begun considering trade as an opportunity for promoting mutually beneficial Sino-Japanese exchange. Under the auspices of JCFA's mission to encourage Sino-Japanese trade, Uchiyama gave numerous talks to businesses throughout Japan, promoting specific products that Japan could trade with China. With his acute business sense, a rich network of Shanghai connections, and innate skill and tact in connecting people, Uchiyama set about facilitating links between Chinese and Japanese businesspeople interested in trading with their counterparts.

Uchiyama's promotion of the lacquer trade is an example of his activity in this sphere. Since 1935, through Lu Xun, Uchiyama and Wu Langxi 吳朗西 (1904-1992) of Cultural Life Publishing knew each other. By 1950 Wu, now with Huaguang Trading Company, approached Uchiyama for advice on engaging in Sino-Japanese trade. Uchiyama suggested that Huaguang consider exporting Chinese lacquer to Japan from a lacquer-producing center in Sichuan Province. He observed that although there was a market in Japan for Chinese lacquerware, prewar China-based Japanese distributors to the Japanese market could no longer operate out of China. Uchiyama personally knew two of the former Chinese-based distributors. Anticipating a future business opportunity, he had already collected detailed information on the Chinese Sichuan lacquer trade from them, which he gave to Wu. As a result, in 1949, Wu traveled to Japan with an East Asia Association delegation of Chinese traders seeking trading opportunities with their Japanese counterparts. Later that year, Uchiyama's idea came to fruition when eighteen tons of Chinese lacquer arrived at the Port of Kobe.

Later, Wu Langxi joined the PRC's Ministry of Agriculture as section chief in charge of lacquer. In this capacity, he visited a paper mill in Niigata prefecture to explore importing Japanese newsprint to China in exchange for exporting Chinese lacquer to Japan. Coincidentally, while Wu was in Niigata prefecture, Uchiyama happened to be in the area delivering *mandan,* and Wu attended a talk on opportunities for business cooperation with China. During the event, Uchiyama introduced audience member Wu as a representative of Chinese trade groups interested in Japan, never missing an opportunity to bring together Chinese and Japanese for business.

Delegates representing United Nations member states gathered in 1951 in San Francisco to draft the Treaty that officially ended the Allied occupation of Japan. On September 8, 1951, forty-eight UN member states signed the Treaty of Peace with Japan.[33] Later the same month, the U.S. and Japan signed the Treaty of Mutual Cooperation and Security,[34] establishing a military alliance between the two nations.

Contrary to the popular image of a peaceful postwar Japan, "peace" in postwar Japan has been highly contested. Historian James Orr[35] typifies those who have portrayed postwar Japanese peace movements as promulgating the view of "Japan as the victim of war" rather than "Japan as the aggressor." The "victim" view characterizes anti-nuclear organizations and organizations opposed to American military bases on Japanese soil. However, "Japan as the aggressor" shaped the opinion of many other organizations.

For example, before the U.S. Senate ratified the Treaty of San Francisco, four Japanese activists formed a committee to oppose Japan's rearmament.[36] These women argued that because the treaty did not expressly prohibit Japan from rearming, it conflicted with Article 9 of the 1947 Constitution. In January 1952, the committee gathered petitions signed by women throughout Japan. The petitions quoted Article 9:

> Aspiring sincerely to an international peace based on justice and order, the Japanese people forever renounce war as a sovereign right of the nation and the threat or use of force to settle international disputes. To accomplish the aim of the preceding paragraph, land, sea, air forces, and other war potential armaments will never be maintained. The right of belligerency of the state will not be recognized.

The formally worded petitions called on members of the U.S. Senate to amend the Treaty to include the statement: "Japanese women hope that the Japanese will permanently abandon armament." The petition concluded with a phrase commonly used by postwar peace activists: "We have vowed never again to send our children or our husbands to the war front." The left-leaning Teachers' Union also vowed: "Never again will we send our students to war." Thus, left-wing politicians, peace groups, and organizations that promote positive Sino-Japanese relations, the oldest and most vocal of which is JCFA, have continued to play an active, coordinated role in ensuring that Article 9 remains unchanged

Between 1949 and 1972, when Japan and China had no official diplomatic relationship, Uchiyama made several extended trips to the PRC on behalf of JCFA. He not only maintained the Sino-Japanese networks built during his Shanghai years but also expanded his activities. Uchiyama's first return to China since deportation in 1947 was in January 1953, when he represented JCFA in a Japanese delegation negotiating for repatriation of Japanese stranded in China after the war. While in Beijing, Uchiyama reconnected with many old friends, several of whom now held high-ranking government positions. Guo Moruo[37] organized a dinner party joined by politician Liao Chengzhi, Japan specialist Sun Pinghua 孫平化 (1917-1997), and labor activist and politician Liu Ningyi 劉寧一 (1907-1994). During dinner, Liu reminisced about his friendship with Uchiyama, which began when he ordered books from Uchiyama Bookstore while a political prisoner in Nanjing. From Guo's party, Uchiyama went to Ouyang Yuqian's home.[38] There he reconnected with Tian Han.[39] The conversation led to the 1955 founding of the Chinese Theater Research Center.[40]

On returning to Japan, Uchiyama described his Beijing trip in a ten-part travelogue in the *Asahi Shinbun* national daily newspaper. To show the Japanese "what revolution truly means through the lens of China," he guided his reader on a virtual train journey during which the reader "saw" the new China through Uchiyama's prose. Uchiyama wrote, "The first thing one notices is that the trains are too clean to be true. There are no tobacco fumes. There are many cleaning people, and there is no opium to be seen." In addition, he observed that the new China had eliminated the "professions" of coolie, prostitute, thief, and beggar through discipline.

In connection with JCFA-related activities, Uchiyama often

hosted visitors from China. For example, in 1954, he hosted Chinese women's movement activists Li Dequan, 李德全 (1896-1972)[41] and Liao Chengzhi during their visit to Japan on behalf of the Red Cross Society of China. In addition, when Guo Moruo came to Japan in 1955 as a representative of the Chinese Academy of Sciences, Guo and Uchiyama met several times. On one occasion, they visited cemeteries where Guo paid respect to those he had grown close to during his exile in Japan. On another occasion, reminiscent of Tanizaki's 1926 visit to Shanghai when Uchiyama had gathered Chinese writers, including Guo, to meet the renowned Japanese writer, Uchiyama arranged for Guo to meet with Tanizaki. Then in 1956, Uchiyama hosted Lu Xun's widow Xu Guangping when she came to Japan as head of the Chinese delegation to the World Conference against Atomic Bombs.

After 1949 and into the Cold War, Japan was a member of the Western Bloc of nations against the Eastern Bloc and served as the West's bulwark against the spread of communism in East Asia. During this period, the fear of being labeled "red" was real. It took great courage for Japanese people or organizations to acknowledge ties with China. Nonetheless, some chose to devote their lives to normalizing Japan's relations with China. Why would people and organizations take such a risk?

Founders of most Sino-Japanese associations had direct personal experience with China or held vivid memories of the war with China. Some felt the need to atone for Japan's military aggression toward China. In contrast, others with leftist political orientations felt a sense of solidarity and affection for the PRC and its people. Other Sino-Japanese associations came together around Pan-Asianism, connecting them with CPC counterparts and their shared ideologies of nationalism and anti-imperialism. Historian of Japan Victor Koschmann contends that such associations brought together Sinocentric Asianists of the Japanese left who revived prewar Pan-Asian solidarity rhetoric such as "same culture, same race."

During the Cold War, JCFA played a meaningful role in steering the East and West toward cooperation. Many in the wide-ranging Sino-Japanese network that JCFA and Uchiyama brought together were those who historian Akira Iriye calls "cultural internationalists." They maintained close personal relationships with counterparts across national boundaries and engaged in intergovernmental and NGO activities. Together, these cultural internationalists comprised a global community that fostered international cooperation.

Uchiyama credited Lu Xun with establishing the path forward for Sino-Japanese relations. Furthermore, he believed that both countries and their peoples would build on Lu Xun's way through friendship networks. Deep in his heart, Uchiyama was convinced that the Sino-Japanese Friendship Movement was the key to the national salvation of Japan and the Japanese people. He concluded one of his *mandan* with a forceful charge to his audience:

> The Sino-Japanese Friendship Movement must become a national salvation movement. Our shoes were taken away, and our feet were bare. The bare feet that took the first steps forward in the wilderness were Lu Xun's. His were the first steps toward saving China. Let us take courage. With new conviction, let us lift our feet and take our first steps; marching forward together, this is our national salvation movement.[42]

In his posthumously published memoir *Recollections from the Past* (*Kakōroku*), Uchiyama declared that Japan, freed from imperialism and militarism, and embracing democracy based on absolute peace, was no longer the enemy of China. Once again, he proclaimed, "Japan and China are inseparable brothers with the same blood running in us." Although Uchiyama undoubtedly directed his greatest passion toward China, a peaceful postwar Japan was also his great passion. He adamantly believed in preserving Article 9 of the Japanese Constitution to protect Japan from ever again coming under the control of its military. He believed that in safeguarding Article 9, Japan could win the world's trust, which it lost during WWII, and deserve the ongoing respect and trust of all the world's peoples.

NAOKO KATO

Endnotes

1 Kanreki is celebrated in Japan when a person turns 60 years old. Kanreki is a rebirth. After living 60 years a person has made five cycles through the Chinese zodiac and has returned back at their birthplace in the zodiac. The word "kanreki" derives its meaning from the words "kan" (return) and "reki" (calendar). In short, when a person turns 60, it is a chance to start life anew.
2 Sekihan (red rice) is a rice dish made from glutinous rice and colored naturally with red azuki beans. This dish is served on special occasions to celebrate milestones such as births, coming-of-age, and longevity.
3 Uchiyama Kanzō, *Kakōroku*, 421.
4 Without explicitly using the word "surrender," Emperor Hirohito announced the surrender of Imperial Japan on August 15, 1945. "After pondering deeply the general trends of the world and the actual conditions obtaining in Our Empire today, We have decided to effect a settlement of the present situation by resorting to an extraordinary measure. We have ordered Our Government to communicate to the Governments of the United States, Great Britain, China, and the Soviet Union that Our Empire accepts the provisions of their Joint Declaration." The Joint Declaration refers to the Potsdam Declaration, which called for the surrender of all Japanese armed forces. After the Potsdam Conference held in Potsdam, Germany, on July 26, 1945, U.S. President Harry S. Truman, Prime Minister of the Great Britain Winston Churchill, and President of the ROC Chiang Kai-shek, issued the document. On September 2, aboard the battleship USS Missouri, Japanese Minister of Foreign Affairs Shigemitsu Mamoru signed the formal Japanese Instrument of Surrender.
5 Ray Moore and Donald Robinson. *Partners for Democracy: Crafting the new Japanese State under Macarthur*, 40.

6 Etō Jun, *Wasureta koto to wasure saserareta koto* (Tokyo: Bungei Shunjū, 1996), 49.

7 Vories provided Konoe with wording for the January 1, 1946, "Declaration of Humanity" in which Emperor Hirohito renounced his divinity.

8 Harry Wray, "Decentralization of Education in the Allied Occupation of Japan, 1945-1952," in *The Occupation of Japan: Educational and Social Reform: The Proceedings of a Symposium Sponsored by the Macarthur Memorial*, Old Dominion University, the Macarthur Memorial Foundation, October 16-18, 1980, ed. Thomas Burkman (Norfolk, Virginia: The MacArthur Memorial: Gatling Printing and Publishing Cooperation, 1982), 44.

9 December 15, 1945, Japan revised its election law and granted women over the age of 20 the vote. Women first voted in the 1947 national election. In October 1931, six women who had played active roles in wartime peace movements and women's rights movements, formed Asahi Newspaper-affiliated Isshikai shortly after the September 31, 1931, invasion of Manchuria by Japan. The purpose of Isshikai was to discuss China and Chinese women. The six women included Asahi's first female journalist Hiratsuka Raichō 平塚らいちょう (1886-1971); journalist Takenaka Shige 竹中繁 (1875-1968); psychologist Kōra Tomi 高良とみ (1896-1993); educator Jōdai Tano 上代たの (1886-1982); women's suffrage activists Yamataka Shigeri 山高しげり (1899-1977) and Ichikawa Fusae 市川房枝 (1893-1981); and Katō Taka 加藤タカ (1887-1979) of the Tokyo YMCA where her focus was improvement of working conditions for Japanese women. Under the 1947 constitution and broad social reforms initiated under the Katayama cabinet, the goals of these women and the groups they represented, promulgated since the Taishō Democracy and before, came to a degree of fulfillment.

10 Under the Katayama cabinet, Japan adopted a wide range of progressive social reforms. The first Labor Ministry was established. The Diet passed the Unemployment Compensation Act, the Unemployment Insurance Act, the Labor Standards Act, the Employment Security Law, the Child Welfare Law, and the Law for the Elimination of Excessive Economic Concentration. Other social reforms adopted under the Katayama cabinet were appointment of the first group of Supreme Court justices, reorganization of the police and local government, extensive revision to criminal law, abolishment of the Ministries of Home Affairs, Navy, and War, and progress on land reform.

11 August 1946, one US$=3350 yuan, February 1947, one US$=12,000 yuan (February 1947), and one US$=39,000 yuan (August 1947). From a Japanese translation of Hong, Jiaguan. Zhongguo jinrong shi shiliu jiang. (Shanghai: Shanghai renmin mei chubanshe, 2009), 19-20.

12 The fabi yuan (法幣元) was a paper currency first issued in 1935 under the ROC and used until the Japanese occupation in 1938. In 1940 the collaborationist Nanjing National Government established the Central Reserve Bank of China (CRB) 中央儲備銀行 Zhongyang Chubei Yingang) which began issuing CRB quan (儲備券). Although initially set at par with the ROC fabi yuan, the value of one CRB quan was arbitrarily changed to equal 0.18 Japanese military yen. By May 1942, one CRB quan was equivalent to two fabi yuan. Postwar, with the reestablishment of the ROC as China's official government in 1945, the fabi yuan replaced the CRB quan at the rate of 200 CRB quan to one fabi yuan. In his memoir, Uchiyama mentions that in May 1942, 1 CRB yuan was equivalent to two fabi yuan.

13 Uchiyama Kanzō, Kakōroku, 312-13.

14 Nishibayashi was the daughter of Pastor Itō of Kyoto Church, who led Uchiyama to baptism. She worked for Uchiyama Bookstore as a shop assistant and for two years looked after Miki in Nagasaki during Miki's recuperation there from a heart-related health problem.
15 Aug 1947 exchange rate US$ to Chinese yuan: 1US$=39,000 Chinese yuan. In Japanese translation of Hong, Jiaguan. 2009. Zhongguo jin rong shi shi liu jiang. Shanghai: Shanghai ren min chu ban she, 19-20.
16 Uchiyama Kanzō, *Chūgoku shijūnen* (Tokyo: Hata Shoten, 1949), 105.
17 Uchiyama Kanzō, *Kakōroku*, 320-322.
18 Uchiyama Kanzō, *Onaji chi no nagare no tomo yo* (Tokyo: Chugoku Bunka Kyōkai, 1948), 86.
19 Uchiyama Kanzō, *Heikin yūsen: Chūgoku no konjaku* (Tokyo: Dōbunkan, 1955), 191.
20 Uchiyama Kanzō, *Heikin yūsen: Chūgoku no konjaku*, 191.
21 Uchiyama Kanzō, *Ryanpentō*, 39.
22 Uchiyama Kanzō, *Shanhai fūgo* (Tokyo: Kaizōsha, 1941), 49.
23 Uchiyama Kanzō and Saito Akio eds., *Chūgoku no kodomo no kyōshi* (Tokyo: Meiji Tosho Shuppan, 1953), 92.
24 China's "National Shame" days: May 9 acceptance of Imperial Japan's Twenty-One Demands; December 13 Nanjing Massacre; September 18 Manchurian Incident; and July 7 Marco Polo Bridge Incident.
25 *The Bible*. King James version, Romans 12:11.
26 Nishibayashi Sumi, Interview conducted by Naoko Kato, May 6, 2010. Tokyo.
27 Masano had worked at the ryōtei in Rokusankaen, one of Shanghai best-known high-end Japanese restaurant, which employed dozens of geishas from Nagasaki.
28 Overseas Chinese Association, Room 466, Marubeni Building

near Tokyo Station.
29 Nihon chūgoku yūko kyōkai (seitō) chūō honbu. *Nitchū yūkō undō shi* (Tokyo: Seinen Shuppan, 1975), 252.
30 China-Japan Friendship Association, founded in 1963 and based in Beijing, is the Chinese counterpart of the Japan-China Friendship Association. Liao Chengzhi was CJFA's first president. Xia Yan and Sun Pinghua served successively as CJFA's president.
31 Postwar, 575,000 Japanese soldiers surrendered to Soviet troops in China and were interned in Siberia. In 1950, after the founding of the PRC, the USSR sent approximately 1,000 of these POWs to China for re-education. On return to Japan in 1956, they were suspected communists and faced years of discrimination.
32 Because of the manner through which their memories had been "recovered" by the Chinese, some critics of the film question the accuracy of the interviews.
33 The Treaty of Peace with Japan, also known as the Treaty of San Francisco, was signed on September 8, 1951, effective April 28, 1952. Forty-eight members of the UN, including Japan, signed it. The Treaty formally ended WWII. Three UN members refused to sign: the USSR, Poland, and Czechoslovakia. Two members did not send representatives: India and Yugoslavia. Three members were not invited: 1) China, due to disagreement over whether the ROC or PRC represented the Chinese people, 2) Korea due to dispute over whether South Korea or North Korea represented the Korean people, and 3) Italy even though its government had declared war on Japan on July 14, 1945, just weeks before the end of the war.
34 The Japanese know the Treaty of Mutual Cooperation and Security as Anpo 安保.
35 James Orr, *The Victim as Hero: Ideologies of Peace and National*

Identity in Postwar Japan (Honolulu: University of Hawaii Press, 2001)

36 The four were journalist Hiratsuka Raichō; politician Ichikawa Fusae; educator Jōdai Tano of the Japan Chapter of Women's International League for Peace and Freedom; and psychologist Kōra Tomi of the Japan Christian Women's Organization.

37 Guo Morou was the first President of the Chinese Academy of Sciences (CAS). He served from the founding of CAS in 1949 until his death in 1978. He also served as the first Chairman of the China Federation of Literary and Art Circles founded in 1949.

38 Ouyang Yuqian was the founding president in 1950 of the Central Academy of Drama.

39 Tian Han was Chairman of the Union of Chinese Drama Workers and the Vice-Chairman of the China Federation of Literary and Art Circles.

40 The Chinese Theater Research Center was established in 1955 by former members of the Chinese Drama Research Society, which emerged in the late 1920s around Uchiyama Bookstore. The Theater Research Center took shape after the 1953 meeting in Beijing of Uchiyama, Ouyang Yuquian, and Tian Han.

41 Feng Yuxiang 馮玉祥, known as the "Christian general" was her husband.

42 Uchiyama Kanzō, *Kakōroku*, 416.

Eighth Turn of the Kaleidoscope

Epilogue

AFTER MIKI died in January 1945, Uchiyama followed the suggestion of his close friend Tsukamoto Suketarō and commissioned a double grave monument designed and inscribed as Tsukamoto had proposed. One day, he would rejoin Miki there. Uchiyama vowed he would live up to the inscription for the remainder of his life—bridge-building between China and Japan in life, then in death reuniting with Miki. Though forced to leave China in 1947, Uchiyama remained true to his vow. He redoubled his efforts and focused on bridge-building between Japan and China in the opposite direction.

Much to Uchiyama's delight, on several occasions after the founding of the PRC, he traveled to China, often representing the JCFA. In June 1959, the Chinese People's Association for Friendship with Foreign Countries invited Uchiyama and his second wife Masano for an expenses-paid trip to China to receive medical care for tuberculosis. By the time the invitation arrived,

Uchiyama had already recovered. Still, he accepted the invitation hoping to receive treatment for diabetes and gallstones. In Japan, there was no effective treatment for either condition. He hoped that China's progressive medical care would restore his deteriorating health so that he could continue to lead the Sino-Japanese Friendship Movement. If recovery proved impossible, he hoped to die in China and be buried in Shanghai next to Miki.

Uchiyama Kanzō died in Beijing on September 21, 1959. At the funeral in Shanghai, Ouyang Yuqian gave the eulogy. Tian Han composed a poem dedicated to the memory of Uchiyama's life. In the poem's last line, he writes that Uchiyama Kanzō and Lu Xun will keep each other company for eternity in Shanghai. In accord with Uchiyama's wishes, he lies beside Miki in Wanguo Cemetery.[1] The characters inscribed onto the bridge from the calligraphy of Uchiyama's brother Kakichi:[2]

> On the left:
> 内山書店創立者 内山美喜子之墓 (Founder of Uchiyama Bookstore, Uchiyama Mikiko's grave)
> On the right:
> 内山書店創東者 内山完造之墓 (Owner of Uchiyama Bookstore, Uchiyama Kanzō's grave)

The Pedestrian Cultural Street on Duolun Road 多倫路 in Shanghai's Hongkou district is an outdoor museum that highlights Shanghai's literary history and memorializes Uchiyama Kanzō. The neighborhood around Duolun Road was home to Uchiyama Bookstore, and many of its patrons lived nearby. The League of Left-Wing Writers (LLWW) founding meeting took place in a building on a lane off Duolun Road that housed the Arts University of China.[3] A bronze statue in the garden commemorates the five League members executed in

1931 by the local Chinese government—Feng Keng, Hu Yepin, Li Weisen, Rou Shi, and Yin Fu.[4]

Along Duolun Road, life-size bronze statues honor Feng Xuefeng, Guo Morou, Mao Dun, Rou Shi, Ye Shengtao, and others in Shanghai's 20th-century literary history. There is also a life-size portrayal in bronze of Lu Xun in conversation with Chinese woodcut print artists at the second annual *National Traveling Woodcut Exhibition* in October 1935. Among all these statues of Chinese literati is a life-size statue of Uchiyama Kanzō clothed in a traditional Japanese robe, although, in life, he wore western-style clothing.

In 1980 the Shanghai Municipal Government designated the former location of the Uchiyama Bookstore as a memorial site. An automatic teller branch of the Industrial and Commercial Bank of China (ICBC) occupies the site.[5] Inside, a small museum open to the public during business hours commemorates Uchiyama Kanzō and Uchiyama Bookstore.

In conjunction with the 100th anniversary of the CPC's founding in July 2021, Tianjin Publishing and Media Group reopened Uchiyama Bookstore in Tianjin with authorization from the Uchiyama family.

Tokyo Uchiyama Bookstore thrives in the Jinbōchō bookstore neighborhood of Tokyo's Kanda district. The three-floor bookstore, owned and operated by the grandson of founders Uchiyama Kakichi and Matsumo, is "the" place to go for Japan's China specialists. However, most customers of the modern bookstore are ordinary Japanese people studying Chinese as a hobby, traveling, or doing business in China. Uchiyama Kanzō's legacy also lives on in the Tokyo-based Japan-China Friendship Association and its Beijing-based counterpart, the China-Japan Friendship Association. Both organizations actively promote cross-communication and cultural exchange.

KALEIDOSCOPE

Each kaleidoscope turn has revealed a role that Uchiyama Bookstore played and exemplified transformations Uchiyama Kanzō, and his bookstore underwent during his life-long journey. With Uchiyama's keen business instinct, he tapped into the vibrant social movements of his time and built a large and faithful Sino-Japanese clientele. A skillful merchant who knew his market, he created a welcoming space that invited lively discussion and provided books that appealed to the interests of his customers.

Cosmopolitan individuals led these social movements, and each movement evolved within the Sino-Japanese contact zone. Therefore, none of these movements can be fully understood when placed neatly into a nation-centered framework. Uchiyama's customers were intent on "saving" their respective nations. At the same time, all were non-conformists and dissidents. Their stories blur national boundaries, reveal a closer relationship between Japanese and Chinese histories than portrayed by generally accepted narratives, and point to unexplored spaces of this and other transnational histories.

NAOKO KATO

Endnotes

1 Wanguo Cemetery 萬國公墓 in Song Qingling Mausoleum Park, contains the graves of more than six hundred foreigners, including Song Qingling, wife of Sun Yat-sen, founding father of the Chinese nation. 21 Songyuan Road, Changning district, Shanghai, 上海市長寧區松園路21號.
2 Two inscriptions commemorate the 100th anniversary of Uchiyama Kanzō's 1885 birth in Okayama Prefecture. Front side: An inscription dated September 1985, from the calligraphy of Uchiyama Kanzō's biographer Ozawa Masamoto. Back side: An inscription dated November 1985, from calligraphy sent by a group from Okayama Prefecture that promotes the life work of Uchiyama.
3 Memorial Hall of the founding of the League of Left-Wing Writers, No. 2, Lane 201, Duolun Road多倫路201弄2號.
4 The five are known as the Martyrs of the Longhua Incident of 1931.
5 Former location of Uchiyama Bookstore, 2048 North Sichuan Road 四川北路2048號.

Main Characters

DURING THIS STORY, many Sino-Japanese visionaries sought to find a path forward for their countries. Those highlighted here play influential roles.

Arao Sei 荒尾精 (1859-1896) attended the Imperial Japanese Army Academy in the General Staff China section. In 1886 when he was a First Lieutenant, the General Staff Headquarters sent him undercover to China to collect information. He arranged with Kishida Ginkō to use the Hankou branch of Rakuzendō as his cover and base. After retiring from the army, he founded the Research Institute for Sino-Japanese Trade (RISJT) and recruited students from Japan to study Chinese, gather market information, and conduct economic analysis.

Guo Moruo 郭沫若 (1892-1978) was a historian, poet, politician, and writer. In 1914, after receiving a classical education, he went to Japan to study medicine but found his real passion in literature and languages. In 1921 while in Tokyo, Guo and his circle of Chinese friends founded the Creation Society to promote modern and vernacular literature and publish the literary journal *Creation Quarterly*.

Kagawa Toyohiko 賀川豊彦 (1888-1960) was a labor activist, Christian pacifist, and social reformer. He wrote, spoke, and worked on ways to employ Christian principles to support the reordering of society. He advocated for women's suffrage and the poor and promoted a peaceful foreign policy. In 1928, he organized the Japanese Federation of Labor and, with Christian socialists, the National Anti-War League. He is known as the father of Japan's post-WWII cooperative movement.

Kaji Wataru 鹿地亘 (1903-1982) was a proletarian writer, a member of the Japan Communist Party (JCP), and a founding member of the Japanese People's Anti-War Alliance, an organization formed during the Second Sino-Japanese War mainly by Japanese POWs in China, with the support of the JCP.

Kishida Ginkō 岸田吟香 (1833-1905) was a Japanese scholar of classical Chinese learning. He pioneered in fields ranging from pharmaceuticals to journalism, publishing, lexicography, and philanthropy. In 1865 he assisted in founding *Kaigai shinbun* (Overseas News), Japan's first non-government-controlled Japanese language newspaper. In 1867, he and American medical missionary James Curtis Hepburn (1815-1911) published their compilation of the first comprehensive Japanese-English dictionary. In 1868, Kishida and American entrepreneur Eugene Miller Van Reed (1835-1873) launched *Yokohama shinpō moshihogusa* (Yokohama News Anthology), one of the earliest of Japan's Western-style, Japanese language newspapers. In 1873, Kishida opened Rakuzendō, one of Japan's first western-style pharmacies in Tokyo's Ginza district. In the 1880s, he opened Rakuzendō branches in Shanghai's International Settlement, Fuzhou, and the city of Hankou — part of modern Wuhan.

Lu Xun 魯迅 (1881-1936) was the pen name of Zhou Shuren 周樹人. He was a leading figure in modern Chinese literature and a close friend of Uchiyama Kanzō. From 1902 to 1909, he studied in Japan. Returning to China, he became a short story writer, editor, translator, literary critic, essayist, and poet, and served as titular head of the League of Left-Wing Writers (LLWW). He wrote in vernacular and classical Chinese. His debut short story *Diary of a Madman*, published in 1918 in *New Youth* magazine, is regarded as the first modern short story in the history of Chinese literature. **Zhou Zuoren** 周作人 (1885-1967), an essayist and translator, and

Zhou Jianren 周建人 (1888-1984), an essayist, politician, and biologist, were Lu Xun's younger brothers.

Makino Toraji 牧野虎次 (1871-1964) devoted his life to the cause of world peace through Christianity. To this end, he was an educator, social worker, and pastor. He served as pastor of Kyoto Church, president of Dōshisha University, and chief of the Board of Education of Kyoto Prefecture.

Masuda Wataru 増田渉 (1903-1977) was a Chinese literature specialist who translated numerous works by Lu Xun into Japanese. Among his translations from Chinese is a volume comprised of letters he received from Lu Xun. Masuda was one of the founders of the Japanese Association on Chinese Literature.

Murata Masasuke 村田正亮 (1886-?) worked in China for Mitsui Bussan Trading Company. He was active in the Shanghai Japanese YMCA. Besides serving as a member of the Board of Directors, he headed the organization's religious section and wrote for its magazine *Shanghai Youth*. A friend of Uchiyama through the YMCA, he was an early customer of Uchiyama Bookstore. Upon retirement, Murata entered a seminary in Japan. In 1937, he established a church in his Tokyo home, which Uchiyama helped him purchase. After settling in Tokyo's Setagaya district, he was pastor of Kyōdō kita United Church of Christ in Japan, which Uchiyama and his second wife Masano attended. Murata delivered the opening eulogy at Uchiyama's funeral in Tokyo.

Nezu Hajime 根津一 (1860-1927) served on the Imperial Japanese Army General Staff prior to becoming deputy director of the Research Institute for Sino-Japanese Trade (RISJT) under director Arao Sei. Later, he was headmaster and patriarch of the East Asia Common Culture Academy (EACCA). Through these positions, Nezu substantially influenced the direction of Japan's most crucial agency devoted to China-related research and cultural enterprises during the first quarter of the 20th century. The EACCA trained large numbers of young Japanese in Chinese affairs, continued and expanded the number of investigative field trips, and published primary research on China.

Niijima Jō 新島襄 (1843-1890), aka Joseph Hardy Neesima, was a Christian social reformer born during the Edo period into an old samurai family. In 1864, despite the ban on overseas travel imposed on Japanese nationals, he left Japan for the USA, where he studied at Phillips Academy and Amherst College — returning to Japan in 1874. The following year, he established the Dōshisha English School in Kyoto, the predecessor of Dōshisha University, and served as its president from 1875 to 1890.

Nitobe Inazō 新渡戸稲造 (1862-1933) was an agricultural economist, author, educator, diplomat, politician, and prominent peace activist. In 1884, he studied economics and political science at Johns Hopkins University in the USA. While a student there, he joined the Religious Society of Friends and became a Quaker. Between WWI and WWII, he served as an Under-Secretary-General of the League of Nations. He also joined with international and reform-minded Japanese in organizing the Institute of Pacific Relations and served as chairman of the group.

Ozaki Hotsumi 尾崎秀実 (1901-1944) was a journalist and a "disguised convert," publicly supporting the Japanese government while adhering to his Marxist ideology. In 1932 during the First Battle of Shanghai, he left Asahi News-Shanghai and returned to Japan, where he continued to report for Asahi, first from Osaka, then from Tokyo. At the same time, he continued undercover reporting to Soviet agent Richard Sorge, which he had commenced in Shanghai. Ozaki was convicted of espionage and executed in Japan on November 7, 1944.

Sakamoto Yoshitaka 坂本義孝 (1884-1946) was a member of East Asia Common Culture Academy's (EACCA) first graduating class. He focused on economics and continued his studies in the USA at the University of Southern California and New York University. In 1919 he represented Japan at a conference of the newly established International Labor Organization (ILO), an agency of the League of Nations, to advance social and economic justice through setting international labor standards. In 1921, he joined the faculty of EACCA. He served as president of the Shanghai Japanese YMCA from 1928 to 1934.

Smedley, Agnes (1892-1950) was an American journalist, writer, and political activist. Known for chronicling communist forces in the Chinese Civil War, she worked on behalf of various other causes, including women's rights and children's welfare. Before coming to China in 1928, Smedley worked in the United States for India's independence from the United Kingdom. In the early 1930s, she helped journalist Richard Sorge establish himself in Shanghai as a spy for the Comintern.

Tian Han 田漢 (1898-1968) was a poet, translator, and playwright who emerged into notoriety during the New Culture Movement. Together with Ouyang Yuqian 歐陽予倩 (1889-1962) and Hong Shen 洪深 (1894-1955), Tian is considered one of the founders of Chinese spoken drama.

Tsukamoto Suketarō 塚本助太郎 (1900-?) worked in China for Shanghai Toyota Textile Mill. An early patron of Uchiyama Bookstore, he was a founding member of the Sino-Japanese cultural salon for which Uchiyama Bookstore would become known. In 1929 Tsukamoto married the daughter of Uchiyama's mentor Makino Toraji, pastor of Kyoto Church, who had led Uchiyama to China. The marriage cemented special ties between the Tsukamoto and Uchiyama families.

Uchimura Kanzō 内村鑑三 (1861-1930) was one of the most prominent pre-World War II Japanese pacifists. Born during the Edo period into an old samurai family, at the urging of Niijima

Jō, he studied at Amherst College and Hartford Theological Seminary in the USA. In 1900 Uchimura began publishing *Biblical Studies* (*Seisho no kenkyū*), a monthly magazine that significantly influenced Uchiyama Kanzō. Each issue focused on an aspect of the relationship between Christians and society. In 1901, Uchimura founded the Non-Church Movement (Mukyōkai shugi), an indigenous Japanese Christian movement that eschewed the *western* in Christianity.

Uchiyama Kanzō 内山完造 (1885-1959) and his Uchiyama Bookstore in Shanghai are the lynchpins that connect the Sino-Japanese visionaries highlighted in this story. He used the Chinese name Wu Qishan 鄔其山.

Vories, William Merrell (1880-1964) of Ōmihachiman, Shiga Prefecture, was an architect, entrepreneur, and devoted to Christian missionary work and education. A 1904 graduate of Colorado College, USA, he hoped to become an architect. In 1904, with the primary intention of engaging in missionary work, Vories went to Japan as an English teacher at the Shiga Prefectural School of Commerce. In 1909, he established Vories & Company architectural firm, and in 1911 founded the Ōmi Mission. His architectural firm designed numerous homes, churches, schools, hospitals, and YMCA buildings around Japan. To generate funds supporting the Ōmi Mission, in 1920, Vories established the Ōmi Sales Company (renamed Ōmi Brotherhood in 1934) to produce and sell skincare products. In 1941 he became a naturalized Japanese citizen and took the name Hitotsuyanagi Mereru 一柳米来留.

TIMELINE

Year	Events	Uchiyama Bookstore and Its Close Relationships
1839	First Opium War (1839-1942)	
1845	British Settlement established in Shanghai	
1849	French Concession established in Shanghai	
1850	Taiping Rebellion (1850-1864)	
1853	Commodore Perry demands opening of Japanese ports	
1856	Second Opium War (1856-1860)	
1858	Japan-US Treaty of Amity and Commerce	
1863	British and American Concessions in Shanghai merge to form International Settlement, later Japan and other trading nations join	
1868	Meiji era (1868-1912)	
1873	Treaty of Sino-Japanese Friendship and Trade	
1875	Dōshisha founded by Niijima Jō, Kyoto	
1880	Japanese YMCA founded, Tokyo	
	Kishida Ginkō opens Rakuzendō Pharmacy/Bookstore, Shanghai	
1882	Chinese Exclusion Act prohibits immigration of Chinese laborers into USA	

1885		Uchiyama Kanzō born, Okayama Prefecture
1894	First Sino-Japanese War over influence in Korea (1894–1895)	
1895	Treaty of Shimonoseki, Japan obtains concession rights in China, Taiwan to Japan	
1896	First Chinese students arrive in Japan to study	
1897		Uchiyama apprentices in Osaka
1898	One Hundred Days' Reform (June 11-Sept 22)	
	Boxer Uprising (1898–1900)	
1900	Public Order and Police Law in Japan	
	East Asia Common Culture Academy (EACCA) founded (1900-1945)	
1901		Uchiyama works for textile wholesaler, Kyoto
1902	Anglo-Japanese Alliance (1902-1923)	
1904	Russo-Japanese War (1904-1905)	
1905	Japanese begin coming to Shanghai in large numbers	
	Hibiya Riot, in Tokyo popular protest against terms of the peace treaty ending Russo-Japanese War	
	China's Civil Service Exam System abolished	
1907	High Treason Incident - mass arrests and executions of socialists and anarchists (*Kōtoku Shūsui*) in Japan	
1908	First in series of 9 Chinese boycotts of Japanese goods (1908-1932)	

	"Gentlemen's agreement" prohibits immigration of Japanese workers into USA	
1910	White Birch Society formed and publishes *Shirakaba* literary magazine (1910-1923)	
	Japan annexes Korea	
1911	Fall of Qing Dynasty	
1912	Republic of China (ROC) established	Uchiyama converts to Christianity, Kyoto
	Taishō era (1912-1926)	
	Friendly Society Japan's first labor union, founded. (1912-1918)	
1913		Uchiyama goes to Shanghai to sell Santendō eyedrops
1914	World War I (1914-1918)	
	International Fellowship of Reconciliation (FOR) founded	
1915	Japan issues Twenty-One Demands on China	
	New Youth magazine launched by Chen Duxiu and New Cultural Movement begins in China	
1916		Uchiyama and Mikiko (Miki) Inoue marry at Kyoto Church
1917	Russian Revolution (1917-1923)	Uchiyamas open Christian bookstore in their Weishengli home run by Miki
1918	*New Youth* magazine publishes Lu Xun's *Diary of a Madman*, first modern work written in vernacular Chinese in the Republican period.	
	Nation-wide rice riots in Japan	
	New Village Movement launched by Musakōji Saneatsu	

1919	Paris Peace Conference negotiations ending WWI (1919-1920)	
	May Fourth Movement	
	League of Nations established (1919-1946)	
	Japan fails to achieve Racial Equality clause in League of Nations covenant	
	New Village Movement introduced in China	
1920		Uchiyama selects speakers from Japan for first annual Shanghai YMCA Summer Lecture Series including Kagawa Toyohiko
1921	Communist Party of China (CPC) formed	
	Creation Society formed (1921-1930). Publishes *Creation Quarterly* (1922-1924)	
	New Youth serializes Lu Xun's *The True Story of Ah Q* (1921-22)	
	The Sowers literary magazine launches proleterian literature movement (1921-1923)	
1922	All-Japan Society for Legal Equality formed (1922-1940)	
	Japanese Communist Party (JCP) formed	
1923	Great Kanto Earthquake	
1924	Immigration Act of 1924 (Johnson-Reed Act) USA excludes Asian immigration	Bookstore moves out of the Uchiyama home into dedicated space in Weishengli
	First United Front (1924-1927) between KMT and CPC	
1925	May Thirtieth Movement (Shanghai Massacre of 1925)	Shanghai *Mandankai* chatting group formed at Uchiyama Bookstore in Weishengli

KALEIDOSCOPE

	Institute of Pacific Relations (IPR) established (1925-1960)	
	Peace Preservation Law in Japan prohibits advocacy of communism	
1926	Shōwa era (1926-1989)	Lu Xun flees south from Beijing
	Northern Expedition of National Revolutionary Army under KMT leadership (1926-1928)	
	Kingdom of God Movement launched by Kagawa Toyohiko	
	Enpon (1 yen book) boom in Japan	
1927	April 12 Incident (Shanghai Massacre of April 12). White Terror period of anti-Communist campaigns begin, ruling KMT splits into left- and right-wing factions	Uchiyama Bookstore *Mandankai* publishes *Kaleidoscope* magazine (1927-1930)
		Lu Xun arrives in Shanghai and lives in Jingyunli
		Guo Morou hides at Uchiyama Bookstore in Weishengli
1928	March 15 Incident, government crackdown and mass arrest of socialists and communists in Japan	Uchiyama doubles size of the Weishengli bookstore
	All-Japan Proletarian Art Federation formed, publishes monthly magazine *Senki* (1928-1931)	Uchiyama arranges for Guo Morou to take refuge in Japan.
		Lu Xun begins editing *The Current*, a journal publishing translations of articles from foreign journals on art and literary criticism
1929	Great Depression (1929-1933)	Uchiyama Bookstore relocates to 2050 N Sichuan Rd and the Uchiyamas move to Qianaili

			Uchiyama opens "Fuzhou Road" branch (1929-1931)
			Shanghai Art and Drama Society founded (1929-1930)
			Uchiyama opens Japanese language school
1930			Uchiyama leaves Santendō to devote full-time to bookstore and other Sino-Japanese relationship-related activities
			Uchiyama hides Lu Xun on 2nd floor of N. Sichuan Rd. bookstore
	League of Left-Wing Writers founded (1930-1936)		First woodcut print exhibit, prints from Lu Xun's collection, Uchiyama's Japanese Language School (Oct)
1931	Five League of Left-Wing Writers members executed in Shanghai		Uchiyama hides Lu Xun and his family in Hanazono Ryokan (Jan-Feb)
	Manchurian Incident		Uchiyama rents flat in Ramos Apartments where he hides Lu Xun and others as needed (1931-1933)
			Woodcut printmaking workshop at Uchiyama's Japanese language school (Aug)
1932	Japanese puppet state of Manchuko established (1932-1945)		Second woodcut print exhibit, Shanghai Japanese YMCA (autumn)
	January 28 Incident (Shanghai Incident) ignites First Battle of Shanghai (Jan 28-Mar 3)		Lu Xun's brother Zhou Jianren and their families take refuge in Uchiyama's "Fuzhou Road" branch
	May 15 Incident. Failed coup d'état by ultranationalistic faction of the Imperial Japanese Navy		

KALEIDOSCOPE

1933	Takigawa Incident, Kyoto University, Prof Takigawa Yukitoki suspended for advocating Marxist philosophies, mass protest and arrests	Third woodcut print exhibit, Qianaili (Oct)
	Proletariat author Kobayashi Takiji tortured to death by Japanese Special Higher Police	Lu Xun and his family move to Continental Terrace (May)
	Japan withdraws from League of Nations	
1935		Tokyo Uchiyama Bookstore opens in Setagaya
		Uchiyama publishes his first book of *mandan* titled *Ikeru shina no sugata: Uchisan manbun (Living China: Uchisan Talks)*. Tokyo: Gakugeishoin, 1935
1936	February 26 Incident, failed military coup d'état by ultranationalist Imperial Japanese Army officers	Uchiyama Bookstore opens east branch two doors from main store, specializing in Japanese medical books and instruments
		Death of Lu Xun (Oct)
1937	Marco Polo Bridge Incident (July)	Tokyo Uchiyama Bookstore moves from Setagaya to Kanda
	Second Battle of Shanghai. Japan occupies all Shanghai except foreign concessions (Aug 13-Nov 26)	Uchiyamas evacuate to Japan during Second Battle of Shanghai, Uchiyama detained for questioning at Tokyo's Hisamatsu Police Station
	Battle of Nanjing / Nanjing Massacre (Dec 1937- Jan 1938)	
	Second United Front (1937-1945)	
1939	WWII begins in Europe (Sept 1)	
1940	Puppet state established in Japanese-occupied China under Wang Jingwei with capital in Nanjing (1940-1945)	Uchiyama, Kanzō. *Shanhai yawa (Shanghai Night Talks)*. Tokyo: Kaizōsha, 1940

1941	Pearl Harbor. Japan attacks US Pacific Fleet (Dec 7)	Uchiyama, Kanzō. *Shanhai mango (Shanghai Chats)*. Tokyo: Kaizōsha, 1941
	Japan controls foreign concessions through the internment of Allied Power nation citizens and the requisition of foreign-owned properties (Dec 8)	Uchiyama operates bookstores in five Shanghai locations including the requisitioned Chinese-American Bookstore on Nanjing Road (1941-1945)
1942	Tokyo Raid / Doolittle Raid. US bombers attack Tokyo (April)	
1943		Uchiyama, Kanzō. *Shanhai ringo (Chattering about Shanghai)*. Tokyo: Kōdansha, 1943
1944	Firebombing of Japanese cities by US (1944-1945)	Death of Uchiyama Miki
		Uchiyama, Kanzō. *Shanhai kango (Restless Shanghai Talks)*, 1944
1945	WWII ends in Europe (May 8)	KMT requisitions Uchiyama's N Sichuan Rd bookstore (Sept)
	Atomic bombs on Hiroshima (Aug 6) and Nagasaki (Aug 9) by US	
	WWII ends in the Pacific (Aug 15)	
	Allied Powers appoint USA Army Gen. MacArthur Supreme Commander of Allied Powers (SCAP) to oversee Allied Occupation of Japan (1945-1952)	
1946	SCAP issues Ordinance of "Removal and Exclusion of Undesirable Personel from Public Office"	Uchiyama relocates to Yifengli off Wusong Rd in KMT-designated area for the Japanese (April)
1947	Katayama Cabinet (1947-48) first cabinet under 1947 postwar constitution	Uchiyama opens Yijian Bookstore, a second-hand bookstore in his house in Yifengli (Feb)
		Uchiyama Kanzō deported from China (Dec)

KALEIDOSCOPE

1948	Red Purge under SCAP (1948-1950)	Uchiyama, Kanzō. *Onaji chi no nagare no tomo yo (Friends with the Same Blood Running through)*. Tokyo: Chūgoku bunka kyōkai, 1948
		Uchiyama sets off on *mandan* speaking tour of Japan
1949	People's Republic of China (PRC) established with Beijing as capital (Oct 1)	Uchiyama, Kanzō. *Chūgoku shijūnen (40 Years in China)*. Tokyo: Hata shoten, 1949
	Republic of China (ROC) relocates capital to Taipei	Uchiyama, Kanzō. *Sonhe, ōhe: Shanhai seikatsu sanjūgonen (35 Years of Shanghai Living)*. Tokyo: Iwanami Shinsho, 1949
1950	Japan China Friendship Association (JCFA) established (Oct 1)	Uchiyama and Kato Masano marry
	Korean War (1950-1953)	
1951	Treaty of San Francisco ends legal state of Pacific War (Sept 8)	
	USA-Japan Treaty of Mutual Cooperation and Security	
1954		Uchiyama hosts Red Cross of China delegation members including Li Dequan and Liao Chengzhi during Japan visit
1955		Uchiyama hosts Guo Moruo's visit to Japan representing the Chinese Academy of Sciences
		Uchiyama, Kanzō. *Heikin yūsen: Chūgoku no konjaku (China Now and Then)* Tokyo: Dōbunkan, 1955
1956		Uchiyama hosts Lu Xun's widow Xu Guangping's visit to Japan as head of China delegation to the Second annual World Conference against Atomic and Hydrogen Bombs, Hiroshima

1957	Hundred Flowers Movement; Anti-Rightist Campaign	
1958	Great Leap Forward (1958-1961)	
1959	Anpo Protests - massive protests against signing of revised USA and Japan Treaty of Mutual Cooperation and Security (1959-1970)	Death of Uchiyama Kanzō, Beijing
1960		Uchiyama, Kanzō. *Kakōroku (Recollections from the Past)*. Tokyo: Iwanami Shoten, 1960
1966	Great Proletarian Cultural Revolution (1966-1976)	
1972	Japan establishes diplomatic relations with PRC	
1979	Economic reforms implemented under Deng Xiaoping	Uchiyama, Kanzō. *Rojin no omoide (Memories of Lu Xun)*. Tokyo: Shakai shisosha, 1979
		Uchiyama, Kanzō. *Chūgokujin no seikatsu fūkei (Landscapes of Chinese Living)*. Tokyo: Tohō shuppan, 1979
1989	Heisei era (1989-2019)	
	Pro-democracy protests at Tiananmen Square and elsewhere (Apr 15-Jun 4)	
2021		Uchiyama Bookstore opens in Tianjin, China, with Lu Xun's grandson as manager (Jul)

Acronyms

CPC   Communist Party of China (1921-present)
CI&E   Civil Information and Education section of SCAP
CJFA   China-Japan Friendship Association (1963-present)
EACCA   East Asia Common Cultural Academy (1900-1945)
GHQ   General headquarters of SCAP
IPR   Institute of Pacific Relations (1925-present)
JCFA   Japan-China Friendship Association (1950-present)
JCP   Japanese Communist Party (1922-present)
KMT   Kuomintang (Guomindang) — the Chinese Nationalist Party
LLWW   League of Left-Wing Writers (1930-1936)
NGO   Non-Governmental Organization
NRA   National Revolutionary Army (1924-1927)
POW   Prisoner of war
ROC   Republic of China (1912-1949)
RISJT   Research Institute for Sino-Japanese Trade (1890-1894)
SCAP   Supreme Commander of Allied Powers
USA   United States of America
U.S.   Refers to representatives of, or actions undertaken by, the government of the United States of America
USSR   Union of Soviet Socialist Republics (1922-1991)
WWI   World War One (1914-1918)

WWII   World War Two (1939-1945)
YMCA   Young Men's Christian Association (Japan 1880-present)

NAOKO KATO

Map of the Uchiyama Bookstore Neighborhood

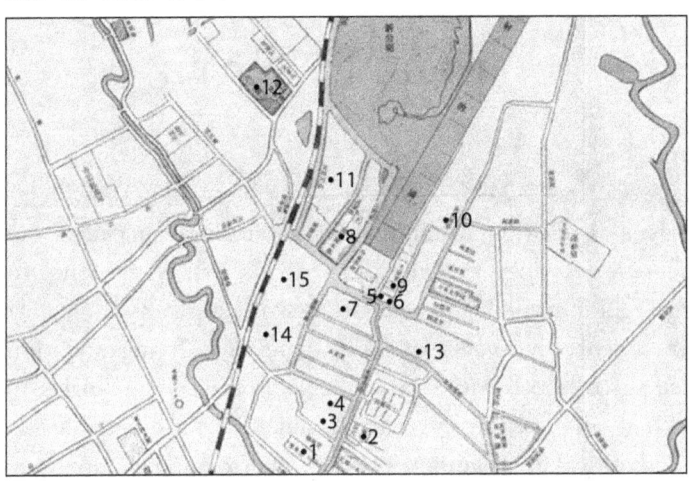

1	*Magnolia Terrace 麦拿里	1811 North Sichuan Road
2	Fumin Hospital, Uchiyama Magazine Store nearby	1878 North Sichuan Road
4	*Ishii Hospital	1879 North Sichuan Road
3	*Weishengli, Uchiyama home and first stand-alone bookstore	1881 North Sichuan Road
5	*Uchiyama Bookstore	2048 North Sichuan Road
6	*Uchiyama Medical Books & Equipment	2054 North Sichuan Road
7	Ramos Apartments	2093 North Sichuan Road
8	Japan Special Naval Landing Force Headquarters	North Sichuan Rd/East Jiangwan Roa/Huangdu Road
9	Qianaili 千爱里	Lane 2, Shanyin Road
10	Continental Terrace 大陆新邨	Lanes 132-192, Shanyin Road
11	*Hanazono Ryokan 花園旅館	Lane 49, Huangdu Road
12	*Rokusankaen 六三花園	West Jiangwan Road & Huayuan Road
13	Lu Xun's "Secret Reading Room"	1359 Liyang Road
14	Jingyunli 景雲里	23 East Hengbang Road
15	League of Left-Wing Writers Memorial Hall	Number 2, Lane 201, Duolun Road
	* = No longer exists	

Author's Note

UCHIYAMA WAS a keen observer of Chinese life. Delivered in a casual style, his carefully crafted stories—he called them *mandan*—described everyday life in China in warm tones to a largely ill-informed Japanese audience. He gleaned his stories from twenty-five years of daily experience living and doing business in the broad swath of Shanghai society. Stories that touched on potentially controversial topics seemed harmless and apolitical to his audience. When interrogated by Japanese or foreign concession police, Uchiyama could always counter their accusations against him by playing ignorant and claiming the harmlessness and apolitical nature of his *mandan*.

Uchiyama painted glowing descriptions of the Chinese people for his Japanese audience. However, consider Lu Xun's critique of such depictions: "The only negative aspect of Uchiyama's *mandan* is that they tend to speak too fondly of China's positive aspects." Thus, Lu Xun concluded, "It is good that the *mandan* are just casual talk and do not draw conclusions."*

While Uchiyama sincerely believed that his storytelling activities supported his Christian mission of promoting Sino-Japanese cross-cultural understanding, he was a skillful businessman with an innate talent for creating stories to support the ideas he sought to promote.

Naoko Kato
Vancouver, B.C., 2022

* Uchiyama Kanzō, *Ikeru shina no sugata: Uchisan manbun* (Tokyo: Gakugei Shoin, 1935), 1-6.

Major Works Cited

Chen, Zuen. "Shanghai ni ita nihonjin: Kaneko Mitsuharu to Shanghai," Media Manabu & Shanghai Virtual Communications Co., Ltd. http://www.shwalker.com/shanghai/contents/serialize/200408/index.html (accessed September 26, 2021).

————. *Shanhai ni ikita nihonjin: Bakumatsu kara haisen made.* Tokyo: Taishūkan Shoten, 2010.

Etō, Jun. *Wasureta koto to wasure saserareta koto.* Tokyo: Bungei Shunjū, 1996.

Fogel, Joshua. "Integrating into Chinese Society: A Comparison of Japanese Communities of Shanghai and Harbin." In *Japanese Competing Modernities: Issues in Culture and Democracy 1900-1930,* edited by Sharon A. Minichiello, 45-69. Honolulu: University of Hawaii Press, 1998.

————. *Articulating the Sinosphere: Sino-Japanese Relations in Space and Time.* Cambridge, Mass.: Harvard University Press, 2009.

Iriye, Akira. *Cultural Internationalism and World Order.* Baltimore: The John Hopkins University Press, 1997.

Kaneko, Mitsuharu. *Dokurohai.* Tokyo: Chūō Kōronsha, 2004.

Kaji, Wataru. *Shanhai sen eki no naka.* Tokyo: Tohō Publications, 1974.

Karl, Rebecca. "Creating Asia: China in the World at the Beginning of the Twentieth Century." *The American Historical Review* 103, no. 4 (1998): 1096-1118.

Kato, Naoko. "Through the Kaleidoscope: Uchiyama Bookstore and Sino-Japanese Visionaries in War and Peace." Ph.D.

dissertation, University of Texas at Austin, 2013.
Kidonikki Kenkyūkai. *Hayashi Hidesumi shi danwa sokkiroku III*. Tokyo: Nihon Kindai Shiryō Kenkyūkai, 1974-1980.
Koizumi, Yuzuru. *Rojin to Uchiyama Kanzō*. Tokyo: Kōdansha, 1979.
Lee, Leo Ou-fan. *Shanghai Modern: The Flowering of a New Urban Culture in China, 1930-1945*. Cambridge: Harvard University Press, 1999.
_____. *Lu Xun and His Legacy*. Berkeley: University of California Press, 1985.
Makino, Toraji. *Hari no ana kara*. Tokyo: Makino Toraji Sensei Beiju Kinenkai, 1958.
Jansen, Marius. *The Japanese and Sun Yat-Sen*. Cambridge: Harvard University Press, 1954.
Maruyama, Noboru. *Shanhai monogatari: Kokusai toshi shanhai to nitchū bunkajin*. Tokyo: Kōdansha Gakujutsu Bunko, 2004.
Goldman, Merle, ed. *Modern Chinese Literature in the May Fourth Era*. Cambridge: Harvard University Press, 1977.
Manela, Erez. *The Wilsonian Moment: Self-Determination and the International Origins of Anticolonial Nationalism*. Oxford: Oxford University Press, 2007.
Miyazaki, Tōten. *My Thirty-Three Years' Dream: The Autobiography of Miyazaki Tōten*. Princeton: Princeton University Press, 1982.
Moore, Ray and Donald Robinson. *Partners for Democracy: Crafting the New Japanese State under Macarthur*. New York: Oxford University Press, 2002.
Nakamura, Shintarō. *Sonbun kara Ozaki Hotsumi e*. Tokyo: Nitchū Shuppan, 1975.
Ozaki, Hideki. *Shanhai 1930-Nen*. Tokyo: Iwanami Shinsho, 1989.
Ozawa, Masamoto. *Uchiyama Kanzō den: Nitchū yūko ni tsukushita idai na shomin*. Tokyo: Banchō Shobō, 1972.
Reynolds, Douglas R. "Training Young China Hands: Tōa Dōbun

Shoin and its Precursors, 1886-1945." In *The Japanese Informal Empire in China, 1895-1937*, edited by Ramon H. Meyers Peter Duus, and Mark R. Peattie, 210-271. Princeton, New Jersey: Princeton University Press, 1989.

Schneider, Michael. "Kōa-Raising Asia: Arao Sei and Inoue Masaji." In *Pan-Asianism: A Documentary History, 1850-1920, Volume 1*, ed. Sven Saaler and Christopher Szpilman, 69-72. Plymouth: Rowman & Littlefield, 2011.

Takatsuna, Hirofumi. *"Kokusaitoshi" Shanhai no naka no nihonjin*. Tokyo: Kenbun Shuppan, 2009.

Tanizaki, Junichirō. *Shanhai kōyuki*, ed. Chiba Shunji. Tokyo: Misuzu Shobō, 2004.

Tsukamoto, Makoto. *Aru jōhōshōkō no kiroku*. Tokyo: Chūō Kōronsha, 1998.

Uchimura, Kanzō. *Representative Men of Japan: Essays*. Tokyo: Keiseisha, 1921.

Uchiyama Kakichi, and Nara Kazuo. *Rojin to mokkō*. Tokyo: Kenbun Shuppan, 1981.

Uchiyama, Kanzō. *Ikeru shina no sugata: Uchisan manbun* Tokyo: Gakugei Shoin, 1935.

———. *Chūgoku shijūnen* Tokyo: Hata Shoten, 1949.

———. *Shanhai fūgo*. Tokyo: Kaizōsha, 1941.

———. *Shanhai mango*. Tokyo: Kaizōsha, 1941.

———. *Shanhai ringo*. Tokyo: Kōdansha, 1942.

———. *Shanhai yawa*. Tokyo: Kaizōsha, 1940.

———. *Onaji chi no nagare no tomo yo*. Tokyo: Chūgoku Bunka Kyōkai, 1948.

———. *Sonhē ōhe: Shanhai seikatsu sanjugonen*. Tokyo: Iwanami Shinsho, 1949.

———. *Ryanpentō*. Tokyo: Kangensha, 1953.

———. *Heikin yūsen: Chūgoku no konjaku* Tokyo: Dōbunkan, 1955.

———. *Kakōroku*. Tokyo: Iwanami Shoten, 1960.

———. *Chūgokujin no seikatsu fūkei: Uchiyama Kanzō mango* Tokyo: Tōhō Shuppan, 1979.

———. *Rojin no omoide*. Tokyo: Shakai Shisōsha, 1979.

Uchiyama Kanzō, and Saito Akio, eds. *Chūgoku no kodomo to kyōshi*. Tokyo: Meiji Tosho Shuppan, 1953.

Yoshida, Hiroji. *Rojin no tomo Uchiyama Kanzō no shōzō*. Tokyo: Shinkyo Shuppansha, 1994.

Zhang, Henpu. "Yoshino hakase hōmonki: Yoshino Sakuzō kenkyū ni okeru chūgoku shiryō katsuyō no ichirei." *Seiji kenkyū* 2009, 127-135.

Photo Credits

Photo on title page - used with permission from Uchiyama Shoten Ltd

Photo on page 7 - used with permission from Uchiyama Shoten Ltd

Photo on page 17 - Source: Tokyo Museum Collection (https://museumcollection.tokyo/en/works/6234773/)

Photo on page 34 - used with permission from Uchiyama Shoten Ltd

Photo on page 52 - used with permission from Uchiyama Shoten Ltd

Photo on page 76 - used with permission from Uchiyama Shoten Ltd

Photo on page 105 - Source: National Diet Library (https://dl.ndl.go.jp/info:ndljp/pid/1872252/3)

Photo on page 125 - used with permission from Uchiyama Shoten Ltd

Photo on page 155 - used with permission from Marcia Johnson

Acknowledgments

I DEDICATED my dissertation, on which this book is based, to my parents Emiko and Haruichi Kato. My mother Emiko has been unconditionally supportive of me no matter what path I have chosen. My father Haruichi has constantly advocated for the importance of a global mindset. His passion and knowledge of Japanese history have guided me throughout my life. My family—my husband Lorenzo, my daughter Emi, and my dog Rocco—have always been by my side during this journey, for which I am truly grateful.

Kate Wildman Nakai and Linda Grove were my undergraduate professors at Sophia University, Tokyo. They sparked my interest in using primary sources to write Japanese history. William Bruneau, my master's degree thesis advisor at the University of British Columbia, and Mark Metzler, my Ph.D. supervisor at the University of Texas at Austin, have been my mentors ever since. They have all continuously believed in my work, and I am blessed to have them in my life.

I am greatly indebted to Marcia Johnson, who discovered my dissertation and brought it to Graham Earnshaw of Earnshaw Books. Together, we transformed my academic piece into this book for general readers. I am immensely grateful for her enthusiasm and support, without which this book would not have been possible.

About the Author and the Editor

Naoko Kato — Author

Ms. Kato teaches East Asian history at St. Mark's College, an affiliate of the University of British Columbia. In addition, she has taught courses on Asian Canadian migration at Simon Fraser University and the University of British Columbia. Ms. Kato is an information resources specialist with the North American Coordinating Council on Japanese Library Resources. Formerly she was the Japanese language librarian at the University of British Columbia Library, where she developed Meiji Japan-related digital teaching resources. Her current research focuses on Japanese-language sources and the writing of Japanese Canadian history.

She spent her early years in Perth, Australia, and Tokyo, Japan. Before settling in Vancouver, she lived in Austin, Texas, USA, where she gave birth to her daughter while a graduate student in East Asian history at the University of Texas. In researching her 2013 doctoral dissertation, "Through the Kaleidoscope: Uchiyama Bookstore and Sino-Japanese Visionaries in War and Peace," the basis of this story, Ms. Kato relied extensively on archival research of Japanese language sources, as well as on her interest in human interactions that transpire within the moral, political, and cultural zones of transnational contact. Ms. Kato lives in Vancouver with her husband, daughter, and dog Rocco.

Marcia A. Johnson — Editor
Marcia has been an active member since 2012 of the Royal Asiatic Society China in Shanghai (RAS). Though her academic training is in the life sciences, since moving from the USA to East Asia in 2007, she has become an avid self-educated student of the region's history and culture. In 2014, Marcia volunteered to lead a RAS-sponsored Lu Xun Day event. Preparing for the event, she discovered Uchiyama Kanzō and the pre-1949 Sino-Japanese intellectual and cultural community around Uchiyama and his bookstore. On walkabouts, and aided by historical maps and writings, she continues to track down physical traces of Uchiyama and his times along the streets and lanes of the former "Little Japan" in Shanghai's Hongkou district.

Since 2007, Ms. Johnson and her husband have lived and worked in East Asia — from 2007 to 2009 in Tokyo, then in Shanghai, where they lead a consulting practice serving China's life science research and development sector.

Ms. Johnson's effort to bring this book to print is dedicated to the memory of the Uchiyamas — Kanzō and Miki.

Index of Names

Abe Isō 38, 129
Arao Sei 22, 25, 160, 162
Barbusse, Henri 65, 74
Cai Yuanpei 100
Chen Baoyi 64, 65
Chen Duxiu 35, 47
Chen Tiegeng 97, 99
Chen Wangdao 58, 74
Chen Zhuokun 99
Chiang Kai-shek 62, 76, 77
Ebina Danjō 38
Fukuda Tokuzō 40, 41
Hirohito, Shōwa Emperor 126-129, 149, 150
Fang Guangtao 64, 65
Feng Xuefeng 96, 106, 157
Feng Zikai 57, 132
Gordon, M.L. 12
Hamada Hikozō 20, 31 (see Heco, Joseph)
Hayashi Hidesumi 108
Heco, Joseph 20, 31
Hepburn, James Curtis 19, 161
Higashikuni Naruhiko 127, 128, 129
Hiratsuka Raichō 150, 154
Guo Morou 46, 47, 62, 64-69, 72, 82-84, 88, 107, 108, 133, 134, 145, 146, 160, 174
Hong Yi (see Li Shutong) 84, 85
Honma Senzō 20
Hu Feng 87
Hu Yuzhi 100
Huang Xinbo 99
Huang Ying 68
Huang Yuan 58
Huang Zunxian 24
Ibukiyama Tokuji 43
Ichikawa Fusae 150, 154
Inoue Mikiko (Miki) (see Uchiyama Mikiko)
Inukai Tsuyoshi 24
Ishii Masayoshi 69, 83, 84
Itō, Pastor 11
Janes, Leroy Lansing 12
Jiang Feng 97, 99
Jōdai Tano 150, 154
Kagawa Toyohiko 38, 40, 41, 121, 124, 128, 160, 169, 170
Kaji Wataru 85-88, 94, 105-107, 161
Kamata Seiichi 81, 82
Kaneko Kentarō 35, 49

KALEIDOSCOPE

Kaneko Mitsuharu 45, 64, 65
Kang Youwei 24
Katayama Tetsu 129, 130, 150, 151, 173
Kato Masano 139, 152, 155, 162, 174
Kawakami Hajime 41
Kishida Ginkō 19-22, 44, 54, 160, 161, 166
Kobayashi Isamu 134
Kobayashi Takiji 86, 172
Kojima Shizuko 70
Kollwitz, Käthe 98, 104
Komaki Ōmi 65, 66
Konoe Atsumaro 25
Konoe Fumimaro 93, 128
Kōra Tomi 150, 154
Li Dazhao 35, 41, 47, 48
Li Dequan 174, 146
Li Hua 99, 100
Li Liewen 61
Li Shutong 84, 85 (Buddhist name Hong Yi)
Liang Qichao 24, 72
Liao Chengzhi 141, 145, 146, 153, 174
Liu Ningyi 145
Liu Xian 99
Lu Xun (Zhou Shuren) 3, 35, 39, 47, 57, 61-63, 65, 67, 68, 70, 71, 73, 74, 78-82, 84-89, 94-101, 104, 106, 108, 110, 113-118, 131, 132, 137, 138, 142, 146, 147, 156, 157, 161, 162, 168-172, 175, 177, 178
MacArthur, Douglas 126, 128, 149, 173
Maeda Tamon 120, 129
Maeda Toraji 42, 69
Makino Nobuaki 36
Makino Toraji 125, 162, 164
Mao Dun 55, 58, 62, 74, 100, 157
Manjirō, John (Nakahama) 18
Masuda Wataru 85, 86, 100, 162
Matsuoka Komakichi 42
Masuya Jisaburō 68, 69, 70
Matsui Minoru 141
Matsumoto Shigeharu 103, 120
Meffert, Carl 97
Mei Langfang 69
Miyazaki Tōten 24, 28, 61
Muramatsu Shōfū 67, 92
Murata Masasuke 43, 139, 162
Mushakōji Saneatsu 46, 47, 50
Natsume Sōseki 132
Nezu Hajime 22, 25, 26, 162
Niijima Jō 9, 11-14, 27, 38, 39, 127, 163, 164, 166
Nishibayashi Sumi 131, 139, 152
Nishio Suehiro 42

Nitobe Inazō 120, 121, 129, 130, 163
Noguchi Yonejirō 61
Okazaki Kaheita 111
Ouyang Yuqian 64, 65, 69, 145, 154, 156, 164
Ozaki Hotsumi 88-94, 163
Perry, Commodore Matthew C. 18, 19, 166
Rou Shi 80, 86, 157
Sakamoto Yoshitaka 120, 163
Satō Haruo 46, 67, 85
Satomura Kinzō 65, 67
Shi Cuntong 42
Shidehara Kijūrō 129
Shimizu Tōzō 69
Shimizu Yasuzō 62
Smedley, Agnes 90, 100, 164
Song Qingling 100, 159
Sorge, Richard 90, 91, 93, 163, 164
Sun Pinghua 145, 153
Sun Yat-sen 24, 28, 41, 42, 62, 100
Suzuki Bunji 38, 39, 41, 42
Suzuki Kantarō 128
Taguchi Kenkichi 13, 16, 28
Taguchi Santendō 13
Takeuchi Yoshio 69
Tanaka Keitarō 84
Tanizaki Junichirō 46, 56, 57, 64-67, 103, 146

Tao Jingsun 69, 88, 89
Tian Han 45, 47, 64-69, 145, 154, 156, 164
Tōyama Mitsuru 24, 86, 103
Tsukamoto Makoto 107
Tsukamoto Suketarō 43, 68, 125, 131, 133, 155, 164
Uchida Kōsai 36
Uchigasaki Sakusaburō 40, 41
Uchimura Kanzō 13-15, 129, 164, 165
Uchiyama Kanzō
  (*see* Uchiyama Mikiko)
  2-5, 7-11, 13-15, 18, 21, 22, 26, 28-30, 39-48, 50, 52-58, 60-72, 74, 75, 79-88, 91-93, 95-100, 106-121, 125, 126, 128-140, 142, 143, 145-148, 151, 152, 154, 155-159, 161, 162, 164, 165, 167-175
Uchiyama Kakichi 95, 97, 98, 132, 134, 156, 157
Uchiyama Mikiko (Miki)
  (*see* Inoue Mikiko) 8, 9, 13-15, 28, 44, 48, 70, 79, 96-98, 114, 115, 125, 126, 131, 134, 139, 152, 155, 156, 168, 173
Uchiyama Matsumo 97, 134, 157
Wu Langxi 142, 143
Wu Qishan 70, 75, 165
  (*see* Uchiyama Kanzō)

Xia Mianzun 58, 61, 72, 84, 106
Xia Yan 57, 62, 87, 103, 153
Xie Liuyi 69
Xu Guangping 73, 78-81, 100, 146, 175
Yamagami Masayoshi 88-90, 92
Yamaguchi Shinichi 69, 70
Yamamoto Kakuma 12
Yamamoto Sanehiko 67, 68, 72, 87, 103
Van Reed, Eugene Miller 20, 21, 161
Vories, William Merrell 128, 165
Wang Daoyuan 68
Wang Duqing 64, 66, 69
Wang Xuewen 91
Ye Shengtao 55, 58, 74, 157
Yokomitsu Riichi 71
Yoshino Sakuzō 38-41, 47
Yu Dafu 50, 62, 66, 67, 69, 71
Zhang Xichen 72, 106
Zhao Jingshen 55
Zheng Boqi 58, 69, 70, 81, 89
Zhou Haiying 80
Zhou Jianren 80, 81, 162, 171
Zhou Shuren (*see* Lu Xun) 57, 161
Zhou Zuoren 47, 61, 161

www.ingramcontent.com/pod-product-compliance
Lightning Source LLC
LaVergne TN
LVHW012017060526
838201LV00061B/4351